Old School Success for the
Millennial Generation & Beyond

ENDORSEMENTS

"*Old School Success for the Millennial Generation* is a must read for anybody who wants to achieve greatness!"

Frankie "The Answer" Edgar - UFC Lightweight Champion
Edgar has spent more time in the Octagon than any other fighter
Fight of the Night (Seven times)

"Just like a world champion fighter needs great coaches, Jerry Gladstone and his new book, *Old School for Success for the Millennial Generation & Beyond* provides the techniques, strategies and mindset to be a champion in life!"

Jessica "Jag:)"Aguilar UFC Fighter,
Former WSOF Strawweight Champion,
WMMA Pioneer

"One of the best reads ever. This book will change the lives of many millennials. It will certainly enable them to stop chasing money and to focus more on chasing their passion!"

Leonard A. Marshall - New York Giants
All Pro- 2x Time Super Bowl Champion

"Instead of isolating the differences which more often disconnect the 'Old School' and the Millennial generation, Jerry Gladstone opens up intergenerational dialogue and does so seamlessly. Jerry offers a new generation the enduring principles and tenets that guided those to the apex of their chosen disciplines; and does this while elucidating to the millennials, their limitless potential. This intergenerational connection is long overdue and Gladstone does this perfectly in *Old School Success for the Millennial Generation & Beyond*."

Tony Ricci, Ed.D, MS. FISSN, CSCS, PES, CES, CNS
Athletic Performance & Performance Psychology Coach

"As a father of two young boys I am always in search of the best way to raise them. I have known Jerry for a decade and in that time he has proven to be one of the most positive, steadiest and rational coaches I have seen in action. Now more than ever In these new uncertain times we are all in need of some extra coaching to make it through this round and the next. Consider 'Old School Success for the Millennial Generation & Beyond' your personal handbook containing a wealth of knowledge compiled by a life coaching expert. You will have all the tools at your fingertips to navigate your way through any situation and find your personal path to victory."

Charles McCarthy "Chainsaw" - Ultimate Fighting Championship - King of the Cage

"As an old school body builder, I hear it all the time on social media. "This new generation can't compare to the generation of the 80s and 90s." I openly disagree. As much I'm compelled to elevate my generations accomplishment and therefor my own…I truly believe there is something powerful in the energy of millennial's. In *Old School Success for the Millennial Generation & Beyond* Jerry Gladstone clearly defines that energy. He's also able to tap into the critical missing pieces of the Millennial puzzle. There is no doubt in my mind, the influential success lessons Gladstone shares in his book will move this amazing generation towards a more empowering, focused and hopeful future."

Tom Terwilliger - Mr. America , "The Achievement Mentor"

"Every generation has their own hardships and struggles. They also have their own advantages and opportunities, millennials are no different. One of their advantages is unprecedented access to information and content. Jerry Gladstone provides the millennial generation with the handbook for navigating life, achieving success and becoming our best selves. I only wish I had this book when I was coming up!"

Dan "Punk Ass" Caldwell co-founder Tapout, President

"The Millennial generation craves mentorship and is eager to improve themselves personally and professionally. Jerry fills that need with real-world advice and practical solutions for this next generation to live and thrive!"

Gabrielle Bosché, Bestselling Author "The Millennial Solution"

"We all know it takes a village to raise a child. However, we are living in a time where the village is reducing in size, and in my opinion, becoming toxic. Jerry is part of the village trying to raise this new generation the right way. This book is a great gift for any young person, actually any person at all. It outlines some old principles the greatest generation was brought up on. It also provides easy to follow instructions on how to live by these principles. I can't wait till the book comes out so I can give it to my children for their birthdays. Great job Jerry and thank you! "

Juan Carlos ("JC") Santana - CEO,
Institute of Human Performance Jc Ihpfit.com

"As Millennials we live in unpredictable times with unique challenges— this book has lessons that help us bring out the best in ourselves, even through this chaos. Gladstone emphasizes that old school hard work, dedication, blood, sweat, and tears are still the secret recipe for success. It's enlightening— embracing an old school mantra with a new school twist."

Charles "Boston Strong" Rosa -
Ultimate Fighting Championship Veteran

"I have had the opportunity over the years to represent some of the most iconic athletes and celebrities including; Magic Johnson, Dennis Rodman, Hulk Hogan, 'Smokin Joe' Frazier and Chevy Chase. Jerry and I go back over 25 years. His approach to life is always so positive and uplifting. He understands and teaches us through his books that adversity will reveal our greatest strengths. Within the pages of *Old*

School Success for the Millennial Generation & Beyond you will discover Jerry's wisdom and guidance of creating and running a top notch business."

Darren Prince - CEO/ Prince Marketing Group
International Best Selling Author of "Aiming High"

"Bae, Fleek, Slay, Turnt Up, Woke, Me Too, #Hashtag this and #Hashtag that, and Selfies are expressions that may have been unfamiliar to many from the Silent Generation, Baby Boomers, and Generation X until recent years. However, for others born between 1981-1996, these terms have become common language used in every day verbal, electronic and written communication. *Old School Success for the Millennial Generation & Beyond*, demonstrates a sign of the times and a stark contrast between reading an encyclopedia to conduct research and with a wireless, hyperlinked, user-generated world, where any piece of knowledge is only ever a few clicks away. Jerry does it again, this time with *Old School Success for the Millennial Generation & Beyond*. This book is bold and honest. As you turn the pages, you will reflect back in time and smile. It's a must read for anyone communicating, influencing, mentoring and working closely with a younger generation."

Duane E. Perkins Duane E. Perkins
Founder & President WHEELpassion, Inc.

OLD SCHOOL SUCCESS

FOR THE MILLENNIAL GENERATION & BEYOND

JERRY GLADSTONE

NEW YORK

LONDON • NASHVILLE • MELBOURNE • VANCOUVER

Old School Success for the Millennial Generation & Beyond
Wisdom from the Past for Your Best Future

Published in New York, New York, by Morgan James Publishing. Morgan James is a trademark of Morgan James, LLC. www.MorganJamesPublishing.com

ISBN 9781642799132 paperback
ISBN 9781642799606 case laminate
ISBN 9781642799149 eBook
Library of Congress Control Number: 2019954738

Cover Design by:
Megan Dillon
megan@creativeninjadesigns.com

Interior Design by:
Chris Treccani
www.3dogcreative.net

Morgan James is a proud partner of Habitat for Humanity Peninsula
and Greater Williamsburg. Partners in building since 2006.

Get involved today! Visit
MorganJamesPublishing.com/giving-back

*To:*_____

*From:*_____

TABLE OF CONTENTS

Foreword		xvi
Preface		xviii
Consider Me Your Coach		xxvii
You're Tougher Than You Think		xxx

Chapter 1	Kick the Crap Out of Your Anxiety and Fear	1
	Fear Is Your Bully	2
	Punched and Punched and Punched Some More	3
	Use Your Imagination to Destroy Fear	4
	A Good Kick to the Head	11
	Feel-Good Story: The Greater the Struggle, the Greater the Victory	12
Chapter 2	Establish a Winning Mindset	15
	Your *Why*	17
	Discovering and Using Your Why	18
	Old-School Warrior	20
	Run Hard; Run through Your Brick Wall	21
	Be Curious	24
	A Productive Mindset Rejects Negative Thoughts	26
	Upgrade Your Affirmations	27
	Feel-Good Story: $400 Million on the Ocean Bottom	29
	The Battlefield Is in Your Mind	30
	Silencing Your Enemy Within: Negative Self-Talk	31

	Like It, Love It, Live It	34
	Old-School Self-Talk: Super Bowl Winner	35
	Old-School Advice from an Olympic Gold Medal Winner	37
Chapter 3	Quitting—and How It Happens	39
	How I Made a Quick Million Because I Did Not Quit	39
	Old-School Wisdom from Muhammad Ali	43
	Time for You to Become a Quitter	44
	Feel-Good Story: An Essay by My Daughter	45
Chapter 4	Your Past Isn't You	49
	Rocky and Me	50
	Letter to the Old Me	52
	Don't Let Anybody Define Who You Are	54
	Feel-Good Story: Jimmy Kimmel	55
	Life *Does* Have Do-Overs	56
	Take Possession of Your Mind	57
	Your Toughest Fight	58
Chapter 5	Setting Your Goals: Milestones and Objectives	65
	The Time for Thinking Is Over	65
	Manage Your Time	67
	Set a Deadline	71
	Use Smart Goals	72
	Make a Commitment to Yourself in Writing	76
	Visual Aids	77
	Pushing through Pain to the Very End	79
	The Ulysses Contract	81
	Rule Number One and Other Tips	85
	Prepare Like a Warrior	85
	Use the Science of Deliberate Practice to Dominate	86
	Best Practices	90

	Newton's "Laws of Motivation"	90
	Newton's Laws	91
	A Bloody Feel-Good Story: The Preparation and Mindset of a Champion	93
Chapter 6	Stop the Loneliness Social Media Brings	95
	Follow the Money	99
	Even Elon Musk	101
	Control the False World	102
	Social Media Apps Traced Back More Than Three Thousand Years	106
Chapter 7	People Skills in a Technology-Driven Society	111
	Listen Your Way to a Better You	112
	Feel-Good Story: Howard Stern	113
	Don't Be Daffy Duck	114
Chapter 8	The Ultimate Gift to Yourself	117
	What the $90 Billion Man Says About Health	117
	The Five Titans of Health	120
	My Personal Story: Desperate for Hope, Sleep, and Peace	123
	To Meditate or Not to Meditate	128
	An Unlikely "Guru"	128
	All Meditation Is Not Created Equal	130
	Define What Meditation Is for You	131
	Substances and Your Health	134
Chapter 9	Building Your First Business	143
	A "Punkass" Feel-Good Story	145
	"Punkass" Mindset	147
	Do Not Listen to the Naysayers	148
	Establish Entrepreneurial Personality Traits	150
	Old-School Grit: Mark Cuban	153
	Entrepreneurial Education	154

Creative, Innovative, and Proactive 156
Feel-Good Story: *Family Guy* Creator Seth
MacFarlane 157
Appreciation Is a Fundamental Human Need 158
Customer Service 160
Create a Business Flowchart 160
Training 161
A Word About Salespeople 161
How to Choose a Business 163
Feel-Good Story: My First Business 167
How to Raise Capital 168
Build a Brand 172
Reducing Risk 173
Adapting to Change 177
Exit Strategy 178
Financial Literacy 180
Personal Finances 183
Investment Advice 185
The Magic of Compounding 188
Don't Believe It? 189
The Data Doesn't Lie 190
Financial Goals and Disciplines 192

Conclusion   You're More Than a Millennial—Much More 199

About the Author 205

SPECIAL ACKNOWLEDGMENT

I am lucky. My beautiful bride of more than twenty-three years and love of my life, Brooke, has a unique and optimistic perspective that makes all things possible. She's caring, devoted, cute, and funny. Brooke, my love, you are my best friend who brings me up when I am down. As an incredible mom to our three awesome children—Austin, a millennial, Allie and Emma, Gen Zs—your compassion and dedication has created a bond of unconditional and eternal love among our family. Hard work, patience, humility, kindness, selflessness, and understanding are the values you bring us each day.

Thank you, honey bunny, for all your inspiration and support with this book. As we often say to each other, the best is yet to come!

ACKNOWLEDGMENTS

Mom and Dad: I miss you each day. Thank you for all your guidance and wisdom.

Austin, Allie, and Emma: You are all gifts from heaven. Never forget how special you are and how much you are loved.

Ellen and Jerry Levine, "Nanny and Poppy": Our children could not ask for better grandparents.

All my family members and old-time friends: I love you all.

Jennifer Hanchey, editor: Thank you for bringing this book to life.

Ethan Roffler of Stories Untold, artist: Thank you for sharing your creativity and talent.

Morgan James Publishing: Thank you for believing in me and for all your efforts.

FOREWORD

Jerry Gladstone says it well when he points out that there are too many "so-called experts" who try to give negative labels to my generation, known as the millennial generation. Jerry has played a vital role in my life as a coach and mentor. He has shared with me invaluable advice on how to attain the levels of success I was seeking. Jerry saw my vision, understood my mission, and recognized the unique gifts inside of me that I was meant to share with the world. His strategies let me go beyond what I thought I was capable of, resulting in a truly joyous life.

As a three-time WBC Lightweight World Champion pro boxer and Hall of Fame inductee, I know what it takes to overcome adversity and hardship to reach a goal. As millennials, we face different stresses, challenges, and pain points than previous generations. Desire isn't enough to ensure we'll achieve; we must have a game plan. In *Old-School Success for the Millennial Generation & Beyond*, you will find approaches, methods, and actions to design the life you desire.

Jerry is the perfect person to write this book. As he told me, "I know what it's like to be on the 'wrong side of the fence,' constantly getting in my own way, going nowhere fast. So, If I can help people use fear as fuel to motivate them to get out of their comfort zone or improve their financial situation or if I can provide good techniques to deal with stress and help create a mindset that lets people start living in the present and leaving the past behind, then it's good enough for me. My goal is to help others 'get to the other side of their fence.' "

You will enjoy reading and learning from old-school success icons and lifelong achievers, like billionaire Mark Cuban, Sylvester Stallone, and Snoop Dog, as well as Super Bowl champions, Grammy Award winners, Olympians, and UFC world champions. In this book, you will discover the pathway to turn your adversities into your greatest gifts, how fear is nothing but a liar, and how your habits and rituals become your foundation to your success.

I hope you benefit and enjoy *Old-School Success for the Millennial Generation & Beyond* as much as I have.

Ann-Marie Saccurato
Three-Time WBC Lightweight World Champion
Boxing Hall of Fame Inductee

PREFACE

As a millennial, you've likely been insulted by members of older generations. The "established order" has come up with catchy—and unflattering—phrases to describe millennials, such as "Generation Me," the "Peter Pan Generation," "Trophy Kids," and "Snow Flakes." More positive titles for your group are Generation Y or Gen Y.

Sadly, many have "written you off" and harshly judge your group, ascribing a sense of entitlement, laziness, and ingratitude to all those born between the early 1980s and late 1990s. But you should not be dismissed or ignored. By 2020, millennials are expected to make up approximately half of the US workforce. According to *Financial Times*, millennials are big news—and with good reason. It is an exclusive club of 1.8 billion people, which accounts for about a quarter of the world's population.[1]

While every generation shares undeniable markers, having been shaped by the social and political climate of their formative years, no generation's characteristics are superior to another. Each generation has strengths and innovations to add to the world, and each generation also has their pain points and struggles. Some may criticize your idealism, but I say it's a virtue. You offer a fresh perspective to those who've gone before. You believe in social justice and making things better and fairer for all people. All generations could benefit from adopting the hope with which you view

---

1   Cale Tilford, "The Millennial Moment: In Charts," *Financial Times*, June 6, 2018, https://www.ft.com/content/f81ac17a-68ae-11e8-b6eb-4acfcfb08c11.

the world. You don't just want a job, you want a purpose. You are more propelled by influence and change than past generations.

You are civic-minded and work for the good of others. You value the team over the individual. Many of your generation are involved with nonprofits and have sacrificed personal gain to help the struggling or underprivileged. You may not be surprised to hear that, as a result of millennial involvement, volunteer rates in the Peace Corps and AmeriCorps are at all-time highs. Others may call you the Generation Me, but your heart for service tells another story. The emphasis on *me* could also reflect the individualism our society now values—versus indicating an empty selfishness that should be reviled.

Millennials also value flexibility. You aren't interested in your parents' nine-to-five work schedule. Instead, you value self-care and have life goals that include personal growth—not just career success. You also prefer egalitarianism over the hierarchical power structures that birthed the concept of "climbing the corporate ladder."

Instead of conforming to a company's idea of success, millennials would rather start and run their own business, powered by their vision of making the world a better place. Though confident in your opinions, millennials are also less likely to be rigidly partisan in political views, valuing connection and dialogue over dogma. Even so, your generation generally sees the government as the key to change, with the "greatest potential to address society's biggest issues."[2] Of foremost concern is pay inequality as, again, millennials are dedicated to making the world better for all.

You also believe in equal rights for the marginalized, like racial minorities and the LGBTQ community. A product of the world you grew up in, you are more educated than any previous generation. In

---

2   "The Ultimate List of Millennial Characteristics," Lucky Attitude, accessed Oct. 16, 2018, http://luckyattitude.co.uk/millennial-characteristics/.

fact, more female millennials have a bachelor's degree than their male counterparts—a definite departure from previous age groups.[3] Your formative years were shaped by the explosion of the World Wide Web. The Pew Research Center even named millennials "digital natives in a world of digital immigrants."[4] Your savvy and know-how with technology is second nature.

All in all, you have some pretty amazing gifts to offer the world. The world needs the strengths and skills unique to your generation. However, there are limitations. Millennials face distinct struggles; obstacles that may make you feel hamstrung in life. Have you felt, up to this point, that my assessment of your generation felt a little too good to be true? The truth is, serious problems confront you as you learn to "adult" in our modern age.

Attaining more education than previous generations certainly sounds like a plus, but 2016 research shows that 51 percent of millennials are underemployed, stuck in jobs that don't even require the degree they earned.[5] And, that degree cost money—lots of it. Student debt is at an all-time high, with 40 percent of Americans ages eighteen to twenty-nine saddled with it.[6] And paying it back might seem all but impossible as the typical millennial earned between $30,000 and $40,000 in 2016.[7]

---

3   Richard Fry, Ruth Igielnik, and Eileen Patten, "How Millennials Today Compare with Their Grandparents 50 Years Ago," Pew Research Center, March 16, 2018, http://www.pewresearch.org/fact-tank/2018/03/16/how-millennials-compare-with-their-grandparents/.

4   Ibid.

5   "The Economic Challenge of Being a Millennial," Virginia 21, September 21, 2017, https://www.virginia21.org/va-21-blog/unique-economic-challenges-affecting-millennials.

6   "The Ten Most Serious Problems Faced by Millennials," BestWork, Inc., https://bestworkinc.com/10-serious-problems-millennials-face/, accessed Oct. 16, 2018.

7   Andy Kiersz, "Here's How Much the Typical Millennial, Gen X, and Baby-Boomer Worker Earns in Each State," Business Insider, September 4, 2018, https://www.businessinsider.com/typical-income-millennial-gen-x-baby-boomers-every-state-us-2018-7.

No wonder so many millennials still live with their parents and are less likely to become homeowners than previous generations.

To cap it all off, this dismal economic assessment is affecting and being affected by looming anxiety, stress, and depression. No other generation has experienced quarter-life crisis at such a high rate. Some say it's because parents labeled you as special and made sure you never failed. Real-life disappointments set in, and you just couldn't cope. Some say social media has made you the loneliest generation, trading likes and posts for face-to-face friendships. And, the proliferation of online pornography has made true intimacy more difficult. The pressure to achieve grew steadily during your formative years as the ever-rising GPA required for college became the focal point of parents, teachers, and school administrators. *Psychology Today* summarizes the chilling result of all this mental angst: "According to the American College Health Association (ACHA) the suicide rate among young adults, ages 15-24, has tripled since the 1950s."[8]

While these generalizations, both positive and negative, may fit a large majority of your peers, every trait I've listed may not feel true to you. You are an individual, and it's important not to rest on the good attributed to Gen Y or be sidetracked by the limitations. Don't let society or the media tell you who you are and what you should be. You have unique potential and specific pain points, and if you picked up this book, then you are likely motivated to overcome your struggles and move toward success.

To meet your needs, I've compiled timeless, "old-school" wisdom that may be just the thing you need to get out of your rut and smash the barriers between you and your best future. Don't be a sheep following the millennial herd. If you are not satisfied with where you

---

8   Gregg Henriques, "The College Student Mental Health Crisis," *Psychology Today*, February 15, 2014, https://www.psychologytoday.com/us/blog/theory-knowledge/201402/the-college-student-mental-health-crisis.

are in life, make changes. Unlock the potential you already have inside. Michelangelo claimed that he did not create a sculpture. Rather, the form was contained within the block of marble; he merely removed the excess, revealing the work of art. Perhaps this is a perfect way to look at yourself: always evolving, always learning, always trying to get better. We will work together to unleash the potential you already have inside.

Consider Me Your Coach

I grew up playing sports. It was the one thing that boosted my self-esteem. School was not my cup of tea, but I felt at home with teammates and coaches. Back then, social media didn't exist, and cameras were for vacation, so no one documented every move the team made. Political correctness was not at the forefront either, so my coaches took a tough-as-nails, old-school approach, emphasizing dedication, perseverance, and a no-pain-no-gain attitude. I'm not saying it was easy or perfect. It hurt when coaches told me I was worthless and literally kicked me in the butt if I missed a block. We ate raw chopped meat before a game and were told to get out there like animals and run over the competition. I had one coach take his college ring, which seemed the size of a kitchen appliance, and smack me on the head to get his point across. I could go on and on with examples of hardline coaching tactics.

But my love of sports outweighed any abuse I took, and in the end, I developed an incredible work ethic and learned how to fight for success. See, that's what you need to understand: life can be tough; it can be unfair; and, often, to get what we want, we need to sacrifice and become mentally strong. We all must develop our own strategies to overcome the anxiety and insecurity that challenge us to the core. Trust me, you'll face plenty of competition in life, so if you're not outdoing others on many levels, you will be left behind.

I don't care if you never played sports or if it was a different experience for you than what I have described. My point is that anything you want in life takes effort, tenacity, and guts. You must take control of your emotions, deal with your insecurity, and eliminate procrastination and negative self-talk. The ability to motivate yourself, handle rejection, and establish a winning mindset is not something that you can do "half-ass." As I address that winning mindset, you will see references to my Rule Number One throughout this book.

Ringo Starr, who played with perhaps the most successful music group ever, The Beatles, and was featured in my first book, *The Common Thread of Overcoming Adversity and Living Your Dreams,* put it well: "We have to get out of our own way. And if we can do that, and stop making things harder for ourselves, I think we'll all be much better off. Don't be your own worst enemy. Be your own best friend."

To keep you moving forward, I wrote Rule Number One: Push self-doubt aside. Take massive, proactive, well-thought-out, consistent action to create the life you desire. You will see Rule Number One referenced throughout this book. Use it as a guide to achieve your goals and overcome adversity.

Rule Number One: Push self-doubt aside. Take massive, proactive, well-thought-out, consistent action to create the life you desire.

Success is about moving forward, gaining self-awareness, and taking charge of your life. You, as a millennial, have a unique opportunity, with access to more technology, knowledge, and modern conveniences than any generation before. But these advantages will only take you so far. It's time to show up and make your mark. I want to coach you through this journey of personal growth. I want to equip you with the skills to take on your "pain points." But here's the thing: I'm not going to deliver my message by tiptoeing around issues or downplaying the grit required to succeed. It does no good to play it safe and keep it comfortable.

If you have skimmed ahead, you likely noticed I ask you to participate, journal, and think. Journaling will be extremely useful as it requires you to summon concentration, clarity, and creativity. Engaging with each exercise and writing in-depth answers will give you a great sense of accomplishment and achievement. If you have never used writing or journaling as a way of getting closer to your goals, you have missed out on a great way to communicate with yourself. Writing is also therapeutic because it slows down mental processing as you get your thoughts on paper—an antidote to the constant, cyclical (and unproductive) rumination worry can bring. After focused journaling, you can then analyze what you have written and revise as your thoughts evolve. You will gradually understand more of your emotions, your situation, and who you are.

As a coach would, I ask for your dedication and perseverance. You may also notice I have sprinkled "feel-good stories" throughout the book. These will remind you that your best days are in front of you. Your generation has limitless potential, and we are about to unlock yours. The role of hope and optimism in your success should never be underestimated. Together, we will train your mind to believe that if others can overcome and succeed, you can too. I've studied martial arts for several decades. Even though I am a black belt, I consider my mind a white belt. This keeps me in a posture of always looking to learn, always seeking knowledge.

I write a good bit about running your own business because I started a business and made millions before I was thirty. If I can share old-school strategies, principles, and lessons that benefitted me and they help you on your journey to financial independence, it's worth the ink. My goal is for you to capture the results you deeply desire. I've spent twenty years coaching individuals who've gone on to achieve goals they never thought possible. I am going to provide you with plenty of old-school success tips from previous generations and wisdom from many well-known celebrities who still remain giants in their industries. I can say with confidence that the tools, techniques, and worksheets in this book have worked before and can work for you. Right now, commit to work and resolve never to quit on yourself. It's time to start living the life you hunger for.

You're Tougher Than You Think

My wife, Brooke, of twenty-plus years, and I have three children: Austin is twenty, Allie is seventeen, and Emma is fifteen. We tell them the same thing I want you to learn to believe: you are a lot tougher than you realize.

Think back on all the tough times you have been through. You're still here, right? Maybe you earned a few battles scars, but you are still intact and ready to go. Humans are programed to endure. Our instinct to survive is our most powerful drive. Since our early ancestors rose from all fours to walk upright, evolution has made you bigger, smarter, and more durable than those who previously roamed the earth. Everything you have been through has served the primal purpose of making you more resilient, wiser, and—if you let it—mentally stronger.

I say, be brave, embrace adversity, and do not run away from your problems. Instead, sprint to the difficulty and fix it. Let your spirit rise. Be courageous and relentless while pursuing your dreams. Be somebody who has a purpose. We all need something to excite us, a reason to get up each day ready to knock down obstacles. It's all about feeling good about yourself so you can hit your potential. Be the person you are meant to be. Be tough enough to change. Embrace the mindset and outlook of, "The best is yet to come!"

CHAPTER 1

Kick the Crap Out of Your Anxiety and Fear

We fear violence less than our own feelings.
Personal, private, solitary pain is more terrifying than
what anyone else can inflict.
—Jim Morrison

Millennials suffer more anxiety and stress than previous generations. Life has grown more hectic; ubiquitous smartphones mean we are never off the clock or safe from criticism. Social media makes it all too easy to compare yourself to others' accomplishments, possessions, and experiences—and come up lacking. Are you sick and tired of the comparison, of wondering how good you can be and fearing you'll never measure up? Has self-doubt, anxiety, or fear prevented you from reaching your goals? I hope you're finally mad enough to put actions behind your desires.

I've been lucky. Over a twenty-five-year business career, I've had the opportunity to sit with some of the most successful people in the world: Olympians, Academy Award winners, Super Bowl champs, big time CEOs, spiritual gurus, Rock and Roll Hall of Fame legends, and billionaires. And here's something they all agreed on. When I asked a very simple question, "Why do some people succeed while others do not?" they all answered, fear, fear, and fear.

Here's what I can tell you. Anxiety and insecurity are at the root of fear—and these emotions are amplified by tweets, posts, and Instagram stories. It's easy to be eaten alive by a constant worry that you don't have what it takes when you compare yourself to perceived competitors or the influencers you follow.

Let's consider the many ways fear and anxiety can control your life. Your primary fear might be fear of failure, but much is contained within that concept: fear of embarrassment; fear of rejection; fear of being misunderstood; fear of being judged harshly. We fear the unknown, change, and physical pain. Our list of justifiable fears can seem endless at times. The agonizing anticipation of what *may happen* can be unbearable!

At times, you likely fall into the trap of assuming the worst-case scenario will play out. So, you procrastinate, stand still, and get stuck focusing on the "what ifs." While you wallow in doubt, your dreams are just that: unrealized dreams. Let me share the cold, hard truth: anxiety and stress are both rooted in fear, and how you handle fear will directly impact your quality of life and whether you will achieve all you desire.

Anxiety and stress are both rooted in fear, and how you handle fear will directly impact your quality of life and whether you will achieve all you desire.

Fear Is Your Bully

Let's begin by conceptualizing fear. Instead of allowing fear to be an unconquerable bully, think of it as an emotion that exists only in your mind, a feeling that can be quelled. Beyond your fears await the opportunities you seek. So, what must you do? Stop dwelling on your past negative experiences and stop anticipating future failure. In other words, stop being defeated by "if only" and "what if." Instead, work proactively to get the outcome you desire. If you find yourself saying, "I'm not good enough," please understand, no matter your age or stage of life, you have the power to change. Chances are, if you are not where you want to be, then you have not created a can-do lifestyle that facilitates achievement and success. And, fear is likely at the bottom of it all.

Stop dwelling on your past negative experiences and stop anticipating future failure.

Punched and Punched and Punched Some More

I didn't start boxing until I was in my early twenties. As a street fighter, I was pretty good, but being in the ring was foreign to me. My anxiety of facing off against another person got the best of me. I was in really good physical shape; I remember a particular sparring match only one week after I ran a full marathon (26.2 miles). Before I even stepped into the ring, I was tired. I was nervous. I had the jitters. Being both exhausted and anxious put me on the verge of a panic attack. Not a great way to start a match.

An old-school boxing trainer told me he could help. Pete Brodsky, who was inducted into the New York State Boxing Hall of Fame in 2018, told me, "Get in the ring, put up your hands, and just defend yourself. Don't punch back." He put me in the ring with the New York State Heavyweight Golden Gloves Champion. The man blasted my head and body with punches that came fast and furious.

After the first round, I was shaken and dizzy. The trainer came over with a smile and said, "See? You got through it. There's nothing to fear now, so go have some fun." This experience was a tough way for me to learn his point, but he was right. Each time I entered the ring during this match, I was more and more confident and relaxed. It's a principle I've learned to apply to other areas too: get in the ring, hang in, and it will get easier.

Use Your Imagination to Destroy Fear

In this chapter, I present two strategies for overcoming fear and anxiety. Both approaches have worked miracles for countless clients I've coached. For the first exercise, you must use your imagination, but if you fully enter in, it can be a very powerful tool to propel you forward. My second strategy will be a more direct, old-school approach. I personally use both techniques, and each has given me a great advantage when competing in martial arts or giving a keynote speech. I will also tell you how one of these strategies was used against me.

Strategy 1: The Wolf at Your Door

A friend once gave me some highlights on what Teddy Atlas Jr. said to motivate his fighters. Teddy is perhaps best known for training Mike Tyson. Tyson was the youngest boxer to win the heavyweight title at twenty years of age. He won his first nineteen professional fights by knockout or stoppage, twelve of them in the first round. Tyson is the first heavyweight boxer to simultaneously hold the WBA, WBC, and IBF championships.

I found it easy to put my own spin on Teddy's tactics and used his concept to coach many of my clients. You may be surprised by what I will tell you, but I want you to trust and hear me out. You are not to blame for the fear or anxiety you feel. What? That's right. Fear and anxiety aren't part of your identity; they are a separate enemy. Let me explain why and how you can use your imagination to separate yourself from these toxic emotions.

You are not to blame for the fear or anxiety you feel.

First, take a deep breath and prepare to use your imagination for your advantage. Next, tell yourself, "Fear and anxiety are not my fault." Now, create in your mind an enemy that is responsible for your fear.

Here's what I do. I tell myself there is a wolf (my created image of my enemy) at my front door, trying to come in and cause havoc in my life. This wolf is trying to destroy me and is going after my family. He wants to take away all my hard work and make me an emotional wreck. This wolf wants me to suffer, so he reminds me of my past failures. He is a slick liar and wants to convince me I am not good enough and can never achieve my plans or dreams. He is determined to keep me locked in insecurity. His goal is to derail me and my goals and replace my optimism with fear and anxiety.

But now that I see the wolf clearly and fully understand he is my enemy, I can spot his strategies. I can realize he is using my emotions against me. He—not me—is to blame for the fear and emotional duress pulsing through my body. But now I see him for what he is. Now, I can fight back. Now *you* can fight back!

Create Your Wolf

Remember, the wolf is strong and cunning. He has taken you down before, and he wants to do it again—as many times as you will allow.

This is your task: create your own wolf, something you can fight. Use your imagination to create a complete persona for the wolf, an image you can see, smell, and sense right in front of you. The enemy you design is unique to you. I chose a wolf because of the years I spent working as a bouncer. I could easily envision a "wolf" coming through the front door looking for a fight.

Remember, the wolf is strong and cunning. He has taken you down before, and he wants to do it again—as many times as you will allow. So, follow my steps to write about your wolf and make him as lifelike and vivid as possible. Then, he will be easy to spot and defeat.

First Step

a. Get out two sheets of paper. On one, write the emotions you feel when you are stressed or fearful (i.e., nervous, angry, sad, self-critical, scared, overwhelmed, worthless, conflicted, disgusted, or jittery).

b. Next, write about a time you've felt defeated by your stressed and fearful thoughts. Get yourself worked up and pissed that you had to feel this pain and suffer these emotions.

c. Now, tell yourself, "It's not my fault; an enemy is out there trying to take me down."

d. Begin to visualize your wolf, your enemy.

Second Step

a. On another piece of paper, draw your enemy. Don't judge your artistry; just draw. I've seen clients draw in detail while others just pressed down forcefully with their pencil and—boom—they had an image in their mind, an image they could see and feel. Whatever your technique, don't stop until you have an image you can grab hold of and declare as your enemy. You need to see, smell, and feel the enemy you created.

b. Next, get mad. Focus on the image until you fully believe *this* is what is trying to destroy you.

c. Now, embed that image within your conscience.

d. Fight back against your enemy.

I have clients who keep the drawing in their pocket 24/7 to remind them to fight for what they want. Some put it on the refrigerator or car dashboard; some use if for their home screen. Many can describe their enemy as if it were a living thing. Overall, all clients feel empowered by this exercise when they choose to fully commit and give their all to making a change.

When should you pull out this paper or conjure your wolf in your mind? Remember this enemy when you feel:

- Insecure
- Stressed
- Fearful
- Anxious
- Unmotivated
- Depressed
- Any negative emotion that undermines your forward motion

Make these declarations to your wolf:

- "No way am I going to let you or anyone else define who I am!"
- "I will not let you lie to me or tell me I am not good enough, tough enough, or smart enough!"
- "I will no longer feed you with negative emotions and allow you to gain strength!"
- "I am stronger than my fear!"

Try this exercise alone first. If you are unable to get the results you want, go through this exercise with a trusted friend. But remember, the wolf is an opportunist and will find you when you are weak. The wolf will creep into your life when you least expect it. Do not feed the wolf your self-doubt, fear, or anxiety. He will only grow bigger and more powerful. Fight the wolf because he is the force trying to destroy you.

Strategy 2: Prepare to Be Perfect

Let me begin by saying, I do not believe—nor should you—that some of us were born to win while others were born to lose. Birth, luck, or destiny doesn't get to tell the whole story. Many factors comprise success, and your determination and hard work are a big part of the equation. I've seen it over and over again: people who came from humble beginnings, did poorly in school, had few resources, and were bullied and told by others they were not good enough—yet they went on to achieve big-time success.

None of us were born to win while others were born to lose.

I have also seen many others who were underachievers, but something in their mind shifted, and they became a superachiever. So, what happened? How can one make such a significant change? I will tell you what they did and explain how you can make the change too.

Those who left their dead-end story behind and crafted a new life narrative decided to evolve as a person. Their circumstances didn't change, but their attitude and work ethic did. Others were seemingly born with talent but couldn't control their insecurity, anxiety, and stress, but they were able to change too. So, pay attention!

Bottom line: show me someone who is successful, and I will show you someone who has worked hard to control his emotions and mindset. This person may experience fear, doubt, and anxiety—we all do—but he also has a strategy that will not let those emotions take control. He may have challenging circumstances, but he knows how to rise above them.

Show me someone who is successful, and I will show you someone who has worked hard to control his emotions and mindset.

So, get out paper and let's get to work. With this strategy, you're going to work hard to make what you're doing look easy. You will no longer be fearful or timid.

First Step

a. Write down all your concerns and insecurities about an upcoming event: interviewing for a job, having a hard conversation with your parents or a loved one, asking for a raise, competing in a sporting event, saying no, or setting boundaries.

b. Choose one event and write with detail; visualize the day you will take on your fear. Add as many details as possible:

- What will the room look like?
- What will you be wearing?
- What will others be wearing?
- Will you be standing or sitting?
- Will the other person be standing or sitting?
- Who will be there?
- Will there be music?
- Will there be cameras?
- What's the lighting like?

You get the concept: visualize *everything*.

Second Step

a. Now, in a safe place, preferably in a private room at home, set up an "environment." Create a setting that is as close to what you anticipate the room will look like and feel like during the event you are concerned about.

b. Details count: dress the way you will dress that day; get in touch with how you might feel that day. Take your time and think it through.

c. This is the most important step: dedicate *time* to preparation in this room. As any good self-development book or lecturer would say, "Practice, practice, and practice some more!" In athletics, we call it drilling. I am telling you, if you perform an action enough times, it will become part of you.

d. Write down what you would like to say and read it over and over. I like to read what I will be saying and then repeat it to myself with my eyes closed. I do this over and over until I own the words. You need to do this over and over until you own the words. Soon you will have a glow because of the confidence you have earned.

e. When you're comfortable, recite your speech using your emotions and actions in front of a trusted friend. Ask for feedback, make tweaks, and do it again and again until you're so confident, you are actually looking forward to the event.

How many times should you practice?
- Do it five times, and you're a novice.
- Do it ten times, and you're still an amateur.
- Do it twenty-five times, and I'll give you semi-pro.
- Do it fifty or more times, and now you're ready.
- Do it one hundred times, and you can teach others.

So, what's the secret of superachievers? It's not a secret. Rather, it's repetitive, disciplined, hard work. And this means you can do it too!

Old-school success tip: do what you fear one hundred times, and you will fear no more.

A Good Kick to the Head

I know the preparation-makes-perfect strategy works because I've had it used against me. Years ago, I was a decent kickboxer and had a sparring match against New York State Kickboxing Champion John Kenny. He was coached by Lou Neglia—a three-time world boxing champion. No opponent has lasted more than three rounds against him since he won his first World Championship in 1980. Lou is a tenth-degree black belt and retired from competition in 1985 with a career record of thirty-four wins and only two losses. He was named fighter of the year in 1984 and was inducted into the Karate Hall of Fame. So, do you think he knew how to prepare his fighter? Yes, he did.

I went to the fight at Lou's gym in Brooklyn, New York. They asked me to wait in the ring for John. As I warmed up and moved around the ring, the lights became dim. The music John used to walk into his pro fights began to play. John was on his way, dressed in his fight robe, and he walked the same path he would use in any big-money fight—for a simple sparring match. Lou lifted the ropes, and John followed him in. He went to his corner; Lou put Vaseline on his fighter's eyes and gave him instructions. Every last detail was prepared so that John would feel and see the same environment he experienced at every fight. Though I wasn't a big-money opponent, he took no shortcuts. He prepared himself to be in the zone. It was only a three-round match, but from the first kick to my head, I knew it would feel like a long night for me.

The experience of going up against such a well-prepared opponent taught me a lesson, and I am gifting the lesson to you: prepare, prepare, and prepare some more. When you prepare like a world-class fighter, the day you dread will not be nearly as stressful as you anticipate.

What will you see in yourself when you get control of your insecurity, anxiety, and fears?

- A person who is optimistic
- A person who can manage his stress
- A person who is confident
- A person who has a positive, encouraging, internal dialogue with himself

Feel-Good Story: The Greater the Struggle, the Greater the Victory

Have you heard of the 1993 movie *Rudy*, which tells the true story of a young man who dared to chase his dream? If you haven't seen it, you need to. This story exemplifies all that we've talked about. The odds were against Rudy, but he didn't allow negative self-talk, fear, or anxiety to sidetrack his plans.

I interviewed the real Rudy Ruettiger for my first book, and he still inspires me to this day. Rudy wanted to play football for his favorite team, Notre Dame's Fighting Irish. Not only did Rudy want to play football, but he also aspired to be a defensive end. Now, the average lineman measured 6' 4" and 250 pounds; Rudy was 5' 6" and 185 pounds. The odds, logic, and reason were not in his favor. He had an audacious goal, yet his can-do attitude won the respect of his teammates, who carried him off the field as a champion when he finally played in a game.

In his interview with me, he described his epic journey:

I decided to try out for the Notre Dame football team as a walk-on. My goal was to outwork everybody on the team. I made the practice squad that just works with the varsity team to prepare for real games. Going up against players outweighing me by more than one hundred pounds didn't matter because I was playing football for Notre Dame! There are people out there that will try and knock you down and tell you things can't be done. As far as I am concerned, you should keep fighting to stay in a positive thought process; a single thought can control everything in your body. The greater the struggle, the greater the victory. Most people allow struggles and fear of failure to stop them. The key is to learn from your struggles and move on. Failures will make you stronger and give you the information you need to reach your dream. Struggle will prepare you for success. Without struggle, there is no success. Focus on your dream and never quit. It is always too soon to quit.

Will you take Rudy's challenge? Will you choose to believe it is always too soon to quit? What was true for him in 1975 is applicable to you today. Don't allow the pervasive anxiety and insecurity that surrounds your generation to define you. Develop a mindset that works for you and leave your mark. You never know. They may just make a movie out of your life!

CHAPTER 2
Establish a Winning Mindset

R ead this quote five times in a row. Let it sink in. It was written by perhaps one of the most famous people ever to live. A man whom I had the pleasure to know and work with, three-time heavy weight champion Muhammad Ali:

> Impossible is just a big word thrown around by small men who find it easier to live in the world they've been given than to explore the power they have to change it. Impossible is not a fact. It's an opinion. Impossible is not a declaration. It's a dare. Impossible is potential. Impossible is temporary. Impossible is nothing.

When people ask why I write self-development books, I tell them the answer is simple: I hate being on the wrong side of the fence when it comes to mindset. A losing mindset causes me to feel down and keeps me from living up to my potential. Not only do I want to turn from such negativity, but I also want to help others learn to overcome.

When I was younger, a constant, unproductive thought pattern played on a loop in my mind, which led to self-doubt, pessimism, depression, drinking too much, bad relationships, and feeling lost. When I decided to put in the work to create the life I wanted, everything changed. I realized that while I could not always control my thoughts, I could control whether I would accept them or not. I started experiencing a can-do attitude, which led to optimism and a sense of well-being—all as a result of simply changing my mindset.

I held on to that mindset and great things began to happen. I became an accomplished businessman, athlete, best-selling author, and success coach. Now, I help others get to the "other side" of their own mindset; I help them open the door to accomplishing great things. I was inspired to write my first book, *The Common Thread of Overcoming Adversity and Living Your Dreams*, after witnessing firsthand the success and power available with a winning mindset.

You cannot control your thoughts, but you can control whether you accept them.

Over my twenty-five-year business career, I've interviewed countless well-known individuals about their rise to the top. World-class athletes, Hollywood icons, and award-winning musicians. None of these superachievers were destined for success, yet these icons have proven over and over again that they are not just one-hit wonders but are lifelong learners, doers, and achievers. Regardless of individual background, gender, ethnic environment, or *generation*, they all share a common thread of steadfastness, productivity, and optimism. They've consistently employed a positive mindset while climbing the ladder of success. And if these giants of success can share these common threads, despite their differences, nothing can stop you from embracing the common thread of old-school success as well.

Yes, as a millennial, you might face negative stereotypes, high student-loan debt, and a seemingly impossible job market. And you might think those things give you an excuse to look at the world through a pessimistic lens, to accept the stereotypes about millennials, and a dim view of the world today. But I say, these factors are all the more reason to establish and embrace a winning mindset *every single day.*

The stereotypes about millennials and the state of the world today are all the more reason to establish and embrace a winning mindset *every single day.*

Your *Why*

Are you a deep thinker? Do you have an interest in really getting to know yourself? Do you understand where motivation comes from, and do you truly understand how to motivate yourself? To bring increased insight to these areas, let's talk about your why.

Deep, deep, deep down in your soul is where your why lives. My job is to teach you to first understand what your why is and how to bring it up to the surface as a very useful and valuable resource. Your why is your deepest emotions; it is personal and profound; it is beyond your motivation and more than just what you desire. Your why is something others cannot see, understand, or take away from you. If used correctly, your why becomes your unique "secret sauce." It will dominate any and all obstacles and challenges that come between you and your goals. Your why can help you through the toughest of times, enabling you to push past your fear, insecurity, or boredom. Your why keeps you steadfast when the going gets tough.

Your why is your deepest emotions; it is personal and profound; it is beyond your motivation and more than just what you desire.

Discovering and Using Your Why

To discover your why, you must first be brutally honest with yourself so you can tap into and understand your most guarded emotions. This may be somewhat difficult for you, but to achieve what you desire, have trust in this strategy and thought process.

To begin, gather a few sheets of paper and a pen. Find a quiet place to relive the happiest moments of your life. Reflect on when you were at your best and went beyond what you or others thought you were capable of. What positive feelings did you experience? What did others think of your accomplishments? You no doubt experienced renewed self-worth and self-esteem, confidence, happiness, and other highly productive emotions. Write down the positive emotions you experienced.

Next, think about times you were at your worst, when you came out short of a goal because of lack of effort, commitment, or preparation. Think back to the promises you made to yourself or others in the past that you didn't keep, times you were disappointed in yourself. Were others disappointed in you too? What were the negative feelings you experienced—perhaps depression, disappointment, or a sense of being less than? Write down the negative emotions you experienced.

The emotions you have recorded, both positive and negative, create your why. The questions you must ask yourself next are, what emotions do I want to experience in the future? Do I want to feel the pain of not living up to my potential, or do I want to experience the joy of great accomplishment? To get the full impact of this exercise, develop some type of visualization practice to consistently bring your why into conscious thought.

Anger Frustrated Inspired Pride Defeated Self-Respect Guilt Courageous Dignity

THE WHY

To help me visualize myself at my best and worst, I keep this why bottle on my desk. Each day, I visualize opening the bottle and sifting through all the emotions it contains. This works as a powerful resource when I feel a little lazy or just don't want to make the extra effort. The bottle reminds me of the positive emotions of success, which I want to relive, and the negative emotions of failure, which I do not. All I have to do is look at my why bottle and past disappointments and the horrible emotions I felt are stirred within. This motivates me to attack all necessary tasks. I definitely don't want to feel those negative emotions again! And thoughts of positive memories propel me forward with the energy I need to succeed.

Once you identify and truly *own* your why, it can become part of your everyday thought pattern, which will create a mindset and lifestyle centered around getting things done. Your why can be used as a success tool, a way to tap into the excellence and productivity you need to accomplish all you intend. You will become stronger, more steadfast, and more committed to your goals. You will better understand yourself and what makes you tick.

Perhaps most important, you can use your why to outlast and out-endure any competition you face—including yourself. Your why will change over time with the experiences and emotions you have. Be sure to update your why as needed, as it will serve you well. This is what highly successful people do. This is what *you* should do.

Your why can become part of your everyday thought pattern and create a mindset and lifestyle of getting things done.

Old-School Warrior

After playing college football, going to a regular weight lifting gym wasn't for me. I had plenty of weights in my garage, but I needed more. I wanted to learn new skills and train in combat sports, and I felt it important to be surrounded by good human beings—not just tough people. They say, "Success starts at the top," and head instructor and owner of the Martial Arts Institute, Sensei Anthony Arango, provided the environment and dojo I needed.

"A black belt is a white belt who never quit."

Arango leads by example, both physical and mental example. The first thing I noticed in his office was a simple sign: "A black belt is a white belt who never quit." It took me ten years to earn my black belt, and there was never an easy step.

Before we enter the dojo, we bow in to show respect and to set the table for a positive mindset. Even at my home gym when nobody is around, I still bow in to make sure I give full effort. During any typical class, a student can yell out, loud and clear, "Warrior!" This cry sets the tone for all students to have a strong mindset and train hard. More than thirty-five years later—and even though I moved to another state—my first sensei/mentor and I are still great friends. Sensei Arango's work ethic has paid off nicely. He runs one of the top martial arts schools in the country, with top fighters and a healthy membership of students.

Run Hard; Run through Your Brick Wall

We don't always act as our own best friend. Most of us don't help ourselves out as much as we can or should. More often than not, our biggest opponent is the person in the mirror. We live in a world today where anxiety, depression, and low self-esteem are on the rise and many millennials are suffering. What we need to do is shift our mindset from one that closes the door of opportunity and only sees obstacles as "brick walls" to a mindset that understands that most walls are only an illusion. As Carlson Companies chairman Curt Carlson once noted, "Obstacles are those frightening things you see when you take your eye off the target."

Most walls are only an illusion.

Juan Carlos ("JC") Santana, a good friend and mentor of mine, is a world-class performance and fitness instructor. He served as the Vice President of the National Strength and Conditioning Association (NSCA) and two terms on the NSCA board of directors and is the founder of the Institute of Human Performance in Boca Raton, Florida. JC and I had one particular conversation that reminds me of the following analogy.

Imagine you are sitting with me one-on-one. We have a goal to change your unproductive thought patterns. To demonstrate and shine a light on the current way you are thinking, I take a hard piece of wood, representing a single brick in a wall of bricks. I begin to slowly bang on the wood. With each loud sound, I say, out loud, one after another, the self-imposed obstacles you have put up. I say things you have been saying to yourself in your current mindset:

- I am not good enough.
- I am not smart enough.
- I don't have the right connections.
- I won't even try because it's impossible.

Horrible as these sound, we say such things to ourselves all day long. This is why many of our aspirations are unrealized. My goal is to help you better understand that this mindset, combined with your negative self-talk, has defeated you. This subtle yet forceful frame of mind creeps up on you and beats you—well before you have given any real effort or follow-through.

When I coach, to further emphasize and trigger the mindset I want you to achieve, I take out a large 8x10 cloth sheet with a brick wall printed on it. I want you to imagine yourself face-to-face with your "brick wall." I want you to look at the brick wall and realize it's really not solid at all. Just like any obstacle, it can be dealt with and defeated.

Be Curious

Now, I want you to build desire, passion, and hope by being curious. What do I mean when I say, "Be curious"? I want you to remember back to childhood, to being told you should not go into a room or look behind a curtain or open a Christmas gift under the tree. What did those orders do to your thinking? I bet they made you curious. Your desire to see what was forbidden was intense. I now ask you, with as much passion as I can, aren't you curious about how good you can really be? Aren't you curious about how hard you can really push yourself? Would it be inspiring to reassess what you are willing to endure? Wouldn't it be fun to do what you first thought was impossible?

Aren't you curious about how good you can really be? Wouldn't it be fun to do what you first thought was impossible?

You must learn to look at obstacles or "brick walls" as illusions. Your mind may tell you it is impossible to break through, but your mind is deceived. I want you to change your negative, can't-do-it thought pattern to one that says, "Yes, I can!" And I want you to believe it. You must push through any make-believe brick walls because the success you seek is on the other side.

To separate yourself from being average, establish a new, dynamic mindset that refuses to put up self-imposed walls—refuses to say anything is impossible. When you make this mindset a part of your very core, you will be willing to take more chances; you will be willing to learn from failure or setbacks; and you will not let the perceptions or opinions of others get in the way of your goals.

Visualize the brick wall when anybody, including yourself, tells you your goal is too lofty. Free your mind with the realization that most things people say are impossible are not, in reality, impossible at all.

Somebody's going to do the things you envision; it might as well be you. And it all starts with a mindset that works for you, not against you.

A great example is what happened on May 6, 1954. It was thought impossible that any person could run a four-minute mile. Then British runner Roger Gilbert Bannister ran a mile in 3:59.4 minutes to establish a new world record. That day, Bannister proved the only thing standing between him and running a four-minute mile was his self-imposed walls.[9] Others became empowered by his success. Now there are close to fifteen hundred sub-four-minute-mile runners.

To separate yourself from being average, establish a new, dynamic mindset that refuses to put up self-imposed walls.

A Productive Mindset Rejects Negative Thoughts

Starting today, try to reject any negative internal voice that leads to procrastination or poor self-image. Understand that great achievement is truly born out of struggle and hardship. Have the mindset that all struggles, big and small, are an opportunity for personal growth. Though you don't fully understand it at the moment, you may eventually realize that the struggle itself, not the result, is what builds internal strength of character. Stay the course, and you eventually succeed. Soon you will be amused when the doubters say to you that they knew all along you could do it.

Your mindset is unquestionably your most valuable possession. When you make a decisive decision to take control of your mind and

---

9   Nathan Brannen, "Only 1,497 Humans Have Ever Broken the 4-Minute Mile—and I'm One of Them," CBC, June 27, 2018, https://www.cbc.ca/playersvoice/entry/only-1497-humans-have-ever-broken-the-4-minute-mile-and-im-one-of-them.

feed it positive, productive thoughts, you are on your way to taking control of your life. Have the same mindset as my friend and UFC legend Randy Couture, who says, "Every day, frame everything positively. Every day, visualize success. Every day, set small goals to get where you want to be—get 1 percent better every day! If you love something, stand your ground. Stick with it! Losses are more important than wins because they are a gut check for what went wrong. You have to change something to have a better outcome next time. When I have an upcoming fight, I see my opponent as a problem I have to solve and prepare accordingly."

"Every day, set small goals to get where you want to be—
get 1 percent better every day!"
—Randy Couture

Upgrade Your Affirmations

One of my favorite personal development and self-improvement books, which I constantly recommend, is Napoleon Hill's book *Think and Grow Rich*, written in 1937. Hill writes productive, empowering affirmations because he believed "a positive mental attitude supported by affirmations will achieve success."

A great way to turn an affirmation into a tool for crafting an ever-more-powerful mindset is to construct it in the form of a question. Noah St. John, best-selling author and keynote speaker, developed this strategy, which he called Afformations.© Posing a question, he discovered, leaves more room for the subconscious mind to build on positivity and potential. In contrast, an affirmation is something you repeat to yourself with the hope of changing your thought pattern to be more productive and positive.

Don't get me wrong, I certainly like and believe affirmations can be very helpful. But Afformations are questions, and your brain is programed to generate answers. By asking yourself a question, you are led to compose a to-do list to answer the question or solve the puzzle. These questions will motivate you. And, more important, Afformations should turn your thoughts into proactive, real-world actions.

Afformations (affirmations posed as a question) can turn your thoughts into proactive, real-world actions.

Here's are a few examples of well-known, old-style affirmations:
- "I am on the path to abundance."
- "I am in the process of positive change."
- "I forgive myself and set myself free."
- "I am in control of my life."
- "I am adventurous. I overcome fears by following my dreams."
- "I am in charge of how I feel, and today I am choosing happiness."
- "I am fully dedicated to growing my wealth."
- "I am grateful to be choosing food and exercise that support my best health."

Now compare how you feel and what you say to yourself after using Afformations (affirmations as questions):
- "Why do I feel such abundance?" You may feel more gratitude.
- "How do I know I am making positive changes?" You may realize how far you have come.
- "How do I know I am on the pathway to forgiving myself and others?" You may feel more peaceful.

- "How do I demonstrate I am in control of life?" You may see you have changed for the better.
- "How am I overcoming my fears?" You may notice you are reaching your goals.
- "In what ways have I chosen happiness?" You may realize you are in charge of your attitude.
- "How do I know I will be wealthy?" You may be more likely to have a game plan in place.
- "How has eating well and exercising made me feel healthy?" You may be proud.

Pretty cool, right? You can use Afformations as a way to get your mind working in a more productive, upbeat way.

Feel-Good Story: $400 Million on the Ocean Bottom

Remember Rule Number One? Push self-doubt aside. Take massive, proactive, well-thought-out, consistent action to create the life you desire. To fulfill those tenets, you must start with the correct mindset. I started my business career in my mid-twenties (more about that later). Early on, I met Mel Fisher, a treasure hunter who committed sixteen years of his life to search for the Spanish galleon *Nuestra Señora de Atocha*, which sank in 1622 off the coast of the Florida Keys. Despite the many naysayers, Mel lived with the mindset of his now-famous quote: "Today's the day!"

For sixteen years, Mel believed that each day was the day he was going to find the treasure. This mindset helped Mel stick it out on all the days he didn't find anything. It helped him face all the people who doubted him or said he was crazy, lazy, entitled, selfish, etc. His resolute mindset is the reason he was able to finally reach his goal. Mel found fortune and fame when he discovered over $400 million worth of artifacts that were lost at sea for more than three hundred and fifty years.

In order to do that, he had to have the "make it happen" mindset—*each and every day*. His commitment left no room for self-imposed walls.

When it comes to your own goals, you should adapt Mel's mantra of "today's the day." Along with a strong work ethic and a productive mindset, this mantra is certainly a step in the right direction, no matter what the naysayers proclaim.

The Battlefield Is in Your Mind

We are all human; therefore, we are all flawed. But what do you do with that truth? Give up? Or, can you take control of your doubt to focus on your strengths? So much is decided in the battlefield of our mind.

Millennials face a myriad of challenges unique to their generation, just as other generations faced their unique set of challenges—and lived to tell about it. Unfortunately, stress is a constant, no matter your generation or time. You can, however, reduce stress and control it. It is not the strongest or the most intelligent who will prosper, but those who have a winning mindset that focuses on strengths.

Don't underestimate the impact mindset has on all aspects of your life, particularly when it comes to taking on challenges and obstacles that arise when pursuing your dreams. *The battlefield is in your mind.* Your mind can be your best friend or your worst enemy. Remember, mindset is the lens through which you see everything; it affects your assumptions, interpretations, self-confidence, and self-esteem. If you don't develop a productive and strong mindset, you will be limited and marginalized. Self-imposed roadblocks and stress will become part of who you are, rather than a temporary state to overcome.

A word of warning: a weak mindset doesn't always look like quitting right at the start. With a weak mindset, part of your thinking might say, "Go for it," while another part—which eventually wins out—says,

"Not today," or, "Maybe tomorrow." Is this what you want? I sincerely hope not.

My wish for you is to dedicate yourself to relentless evolution, always moving closer to a consistent and commanding mindset that generates mental power. Then you will be ready to take on any and all obstacles or setbacks. Make your personal development a lifelong responsibility and a gift to yourself, and always maintain a winning mindset.

Silencing Your Enemy Within: Negative Self-Talk

Perhaps the lyrics to "Take it Easy," written by Jackson Browne and Glenn Frey of the Eagles, say it best: "Don't let the sound of your own wheels drive you crazy."

After writing my book *The Common Thread of Overcoming Adversity and Living Your Dreams*, people have often asked me, "What do superachievers you interview have that I don't have?" The answer is nothing; however, they do something that you don't do but need to: they silence the negative self-talk.

I would love for you to have a positive mindset that leads to unshakable confidence and a strong belief in yourself. So, what can get in your way? Negative self-talk, which is an active state of mind that reduces your certainty in yourself and your abilities. All too often, negative self-talk manifests itself in your mind—and eventually in your body—resulting in sadness, anxiety, lackluster performance, and even illness.

One of the biggest factors in my success is my refusal to indulge in negative self-talk. People who quit have given in to negative self-talk. They've allowed self-defeating internal chatter to dramatically affect performance and outlook.

Though your internal voice is difficult and sometimes seems impossible to control, you can control it. You are the boss of your inner voice. When you allow it to condemn and criticize, it can create self-doubt, fear, anxiety, procrastination, and hesitation. Without question, it can destroy your goals and dreams. It's a weapon you create and then use against yourself.

If I were to tell you to be hyperfocused and have only one priority, it would be to stop the hate speech you direct at yourself. That's how crucial positive self-talk is to your success!

Let me give you an example of what so many of us do. We come up with a great thought, an awesome idea, or the next $1 million app. But what happens? Within seconds, we go from extreme optimism to reciting a laundry list of reasons why something can't happen: I can't accomplish that beautiful dream; I am not good enough, smart enough, or pretty enough; I don't have the right contacts; people will laugh at me; I will fail. With negative thoughts driving the bus, you go from being sky high to defeat in less than a minute. And this is why people say your biggest opponent is yourself. Can you triumph over self-imposed limitations?

I often tell my clients to imagine me saying to them the things they say to themselves on a daily basis: the discouragement, the lies, the "logical" reasons to give up on a dream. Chances are, you would want to punch me in the face. Yet, people do speak hatefully and disrespectfully to themselves day in and day out.

Your biggest opponent is yourself, your self-imposed limitations.

The National Science Foundation estimates that the average person has over fifty thousand thoughts per day: "The vast majority of them are pure nonsense. We often dwell in the past or the future, obsessing about mistakes we might have made, battling guilt, planning ahead, or worrying. We are constantly drifting into fantasy, fiction, and negativity. Consequently, an absolute minuscule number of our thoughts are actually focused on what is truly important and real: the present moment. The moment is all that is, ever was, and will be. Everything else is elusive and illusory, particularly as our subjective awareness and feelings are concerned."[10]

---

10 "Counting Thoughts, Part 1," Exploring the Problem Space, January 1, 2017, https://www.exploringtheproblemspace.com/new-blog/2017/1/1/counting-thoughts-part-i.

Discouraging internal dialogue stems from our little brain that only weighs three pounds. Yet, the brain is powerful as it drives unproductive self-talk that can lead you to believe that you have limited or no options. Your self-defeat, depression, and hopelessness begins as soon you believe you are destined for failure.

You are not defined by your past, unless
you allow it to define you.

The good news is, you can relieve your negative self-talk and instead build the habit of encouraging yourself. You can let go of resentments, jealousy, and regrets. You can forgive yourself and others. Remember, lugging the past on your shoulders will only weigh you down and impede your progress. Recognize how much more you have to offer than your perceived weaknesses: your past setbacks, your financial limitations, your physical appearance, or anything else that troubles you. Keep in mind that self-doubt and low self-esteem are dream killers. You are not defined by your past, unless you allow it to define you. Do not build your identity around past regrets or perceived shortcomings. If you do so, your inner critic will control your life.

If you've allowed self-defeating thoughts to hijack your dreams, it's time to stop and declare a moratorium on this self-imposed destructive behavior.

Like It, Love It, Live It

Let your mind envision your best self. Let your darkest moments create a new, better you. It's your choice how far you want to go to get what you want. You have three choices: *like it, love it, or live it.*

If you *like* something but give little or no effort to the outcome, you will get limited results at best.

If you *love* something but don't commit 100 percent, you will have plenty of desire for a favorable result but you're going to fall short of becoming a master.

If you *live* what you desire, embracing a lifestyle of achievement and success, you greatly increase your odds of realizing your goals.

Eliminate any and all excuses from your vocabulary and your mind. They are useless. Don't put yourself under a microscope day in and day out. Instead, evaluate yourself every few months. Ask, am I better than I was? Am I closer to my goal? Forget who you think the competition is. You are competing against yourself alone.

Do things when you are in the best mindset. For example, when I write a book, I only write when I am in a calm, creative place. I don't push it. At times I can write five minutes; other times, I can spend five hours. I have deadlines, but I also want to make sure I am in a place to give it my all.

Action Changes All: Being Proactive Wins the Game

- Don't have ideas? Make a game plan.
- Don't have ambitions? Form strategies.
- Don't have wishes? Take action.
- Don't have intentions? Commit to follow through.

Others may help, but nobody is going to do it for you. Get out of your own way and get it done!

Old-School Self-Talk: Super Bowl Winner

As a kid growing up in New York, my Sunday afternoons were all about watching New York Giants football with my dad. I've always loved and played football. For me football became a mirror of life. The game teaches and reinforces all sorts of values: dedication, integrity, hard work, how to win and lose, and so much more. As a defensive lineman, I was constantly transfixed by the performance of the Big Blue's defensive end, number seventy, Leonard Marshall. His intensity and sheer physicality impressed me throughout his career in the NFL. Leonard was not only a great player, three-time All Pro, and two-time Super Bowl winner, but he also consistently displayed a high level of sportsmanship.

As an adult, I met Leonard in Florida, and we became fast friends. I soon realized he did indeed have strong character, and I believe what he says to himself makes him who he is—both on and off the playing field. It's hard to believe this mountain of a man experienced racism and was once told by his teacher, "You won't amount to anything." But Leonard didn't believe her words. He told me a bit about his experience and mindset:

> Since then, any negative thing I hear only motivates me more. What that teacher said still motivates me every single day to be the best that I can be. I focused on looking around and seeing the guy I did not want to become, rather than the guy I wanted to be. I didn't want to become the guy on the corner—the bum with his hand out, looking for excuses rather than solutions. Forget about everybody else's life; focus on yours. Never be the guy who says, "I can't!"

Moral of the story: you can use injustice as an excuse or as fuel; it's your choice. I suggest you nurture that quiet storm of rage inside your soul in a way that will bring out your very best.

What Will You See in Yourself with a Winning Mindset?

- A person who is optimistic about their future.
- A person who accepts setbacks so they can learn.

- A person who embraces challenges.
- A person who replaces excuses with action.
- A person who is accountable for their own success.
- A person who is willing to go the extra mile to finish the task.
- A person who sacrifices joyful times for necessary responsibilities.
- A person who makes productive habits a lifestyle.
- A person who is resilient, resourceful, and willing to help others.
- A person who does not let their past drag them down.
- A person who never thinks of themselves as a failure (even if they fail).
- A person who has a positive, encouraging, internal dialogue.

Old-School Advice from an Olympic Gold Medal Winner

When I interviewed the 1980 Olympic gold medal winner Mike Eruzione—captain of the "Miracle on Ice" team—he stressed how important it is to win the battle in your mind. Mike scored the winning goal against the highly favored Soviets. His advice? "You need to develop an attitude that recognizes that you are in control of your own destiny. You can't worry about what other people think. For me, it was about practicing. That's the key to succeeding in athletics, school, or business. It comes down to this: if you are not prepared, you will not be successful."

My dad told me something similar, and I have always kept it in mind: "If you understand the value of work, someday you'll be successful. It might not be next month or next year, but what you accomplish will be because of the hard work, not because you were lucky."

CHAPTER 3
Quitting—and How It Happens

How I Made a Quick Million Because I Did Not Quit

Speaking of inspiration, let's talk about how not quitting enabled me to make a "quick" million. By the time I was thirty years old, I was several years into a successful business and had become one of the country's leading animation art dealers, with many licenses and distribution agreements in place with the likes of Warner Brothers, Hanna-Barbera Productions Inc., and Universal Pictures. We had also landed deals to work with legendary cartoon directors Chuck Jones and Friz Freleng. The only missing piece for us was The Walt Disney Company.

For more than three years, I did my best to secure an agreement with Disney. Every call I made was ignored. I had a pile of rejection letters sitting on my desk year after year. Along the way, I found out that a competing dealer did all he could to keep us off the Disney art program. He did not want the competition, so he took advantage of having friends in high places and used nasty tactics to discourage Disney from working with us.

I will never forget running into one of Disney's executives at a trade show. I asked her what it would take for my company to get on the Disney art program. She bared her teeth, just like a real Disney villain—a cross between Maleficent and Cruella de Vil—and snarled, "You will never get on the Disney program!" I politely walked away, but I didn't quit or give up. A Disney license would mean millions of dollars to our organization, so I continued putting my efforts toward securing a deal.

Years later—yes, years—I finally tracked down a Disney executive who could potentially help us. He said if I wanted Disney art then I should consider opening a gallery in Boston because they had no dealers there. I was currently operating my business out of New York and had no interest in opening up a store in Boston. But the day after he hinted that I could get on their program if I did, I hopped on a plane and flew to Boston to find the best location on Newbury Street.

From a Boston pay phone (no cell phones back then), I dialed the Disney executive and told him confidently where I was. With a big laugh he said, "If you have that type of passion and no-quit attitude, then we need you on the Disney art program!" And just like that, my years of effort finally paid off. Within six months, we became the largest dealer of Disney animation art in the United States. We maintained that achievement for more than fifteen years, and I was eventually asked to serve on the Disney animation art advisory board. Passion, persistence, and a refusal to quit paid off—big-time!

Quit. Quitting. Quitter. Words that get you nowhere fast. So why do many people accept quitting as a part of life? Statistics for keeping New Year's resolutions prove that people who start the year trying to make significant changes will most likely simply quit. In fact, people take bets on how long they will last trying to institute a change. When they give up, they laugh as if it's no big deal to quit, as if quitting was their fate.

With quitting being such an accepted part of society—and so detrimental to a winning mindset—let's tackle it head-on and talk about how it happens and what you can do to stamp it out of your life. The tricky thing about quitting is that it doesn't happen in one day, one month, or one year. Instead, it creeps into your life through a subtle but consistent flow of negativity. Over time, negative thoughts lead you to believe you will never accomplish anything. Before long, you are in a losing mindset—not where you want to be.

Quitting creeps into your life through a subtle
but consistent flow of negativity.

So, let's talk about two ways that quitting happens. The first is by listening to others who plant seeds of doubt. People do this for all kinds of reasons—and many times without malicious intent. Doubt may come from those closest to you, masked as worry and concern. Their own fear of failure is subconsciously projected onto you. Though these loved ones should be supporting you and your winning mindset, they inadvertently communicate doubt.

At other times, people throw shade or cut you down to make themselves feel better about their own shortcomings. They may not be consciously seeking to undermine you, but through their words and projected doubts, they make you feel like you're limited and incapable of achieving anything. Their doubt is really a reflection of their own inability to accomplish their goals. After all, if you succeed, they will feel even more inadequate.

It can be challenging to keep proper perspective in the moment—especially when doubt is coming from a loved one—but in those situations, you must distance yourself from any who do not bring positive, encouraging, optimistic emotions into your life. This can be easier said than done. If it's a family member, you may not be able to distance yourself completely, but you can set a boundary. For example, you could tell the close friend or family member that you'd rather not talk about your new project when you are together. You can let the other person know topics that are healthy for you and conversations you'd rather not have.

Even with boundaries in place, you will likely need to remind yourself over and over not to listen to their negativity and to protect your positive mindset. After all, if you fall victim to their doubt, you will become the quitter they are encouraging you to be.

So, the influence of others is the first way quitting can happen. The second fast track to quitting can be even more challenging to defeat; it is your own internal critic. Do you have a critical part that recites over and over again the list of reasons you can't succeed and should give up? That sort of constant, internal, negative self-talk will slowly wear you down and cause you to quit something you once truly believed in.

Therefore, I beg you to always remember, you don't have to let the critic be in control. You have healthy, positive, determined parts who can silence the critic and keep you on the path to success.

Whether the criticism begins externally or internally, the end result will be quitting on yourself and forsaking your dreams. This isn't what I want for you, but it is exactly what the naysayers and the competition want.

Starting today, you must stop flooding your brain with self-imposed words of destruction. Instead, focus on the abundance of reasons to be optimistic. Think on the reasons you can succeed, and certainly focus on the reasons you should not quit. When you get your butt kicked, face a setback, or come up against an obstacle, you need to dust yourself off, learn from the experience, and move forward.

If you are part of the millennial generation, you may be young now, but many of my clients are middle-aged, and when we talk about life's regrets, at the top of their list are the times when they quit on themselves. Even years later, they remember the times they gave up or quit on something they believed in. You don't want to be full of regret at the halfway mark in life. It's a heavy burden to carry.

It's common sense that if you quit, you cannot succeed. But I feel the need to spell that out for you and for many of my clients. Quitting directly opposes success! So, you must train yourself not to quit by remaining optimistic, staying the course, and surrounding yourself with individuals who will help you cross the finish line.

Old-School Wisdom from Muhammad Ali

Muhammad Ali, is, perhaps, one of the most famous sports figures ever to live. I had several business meetings with the champ. After our last get together, a few years before his death, I had a surreal moment. I was asked to help the champ to his car. What an honor and a privilege.

As we walked, Ali leaned into my body for support, and I could feel the power and strength he still possessed. Physically, he wasn't the man he once was, but his life's spirit was still easily felt. Ali, who was bullied as a child, became champion of the world and evolved into an iconic humanitarian. He would tell you to run through your obstacles, to run through you self-imposed roadblocks. Here is a sampling of the wisdom he shared on achieving success:[11]

- "I hated every minute of training, but I said, 'Don't quit. Suffer now and live the rest of your life as a champion.' "
- "He who is not courageous enough to take risks will accomplish nothing in life."
- "Only a man who knows what it is like to be defeated can reach down to the bottom of his soul and come up with the extra ounce of power it takes to win when the match is even."
- "If they can make penicillin out of moldy bread, they can sure make something out of you."

---

11 "30 of Muhammad Ali's Best Quotes," *USA Today*, June 3, 2016, https://www.usatoday.com/story/sports/boxing/2016/06/03/muhammad-ali-best-quotes-boxing/85370850/.

Time for You to Become a Quitter

It may be surprising that I am telling you to quit. But it's time to change the rules of your life. Quitting unproductive thoughts, habits, and worry is just what the doctor ordered. Look at this through a reverse-engineering lens. Examine and analyze what has been holding you back and then do the opposite.

Becoming a Quitter Checklist:

- [ ] Quit trying to please everyone.
- [ ] Quit fearing change.
- [ ] Quit making minor things into major disappointments.
- [ ] Quit living in the past.
- [ ] Quit putting yourself down.
- [ ] Quit letting others put you down.
- [ ] Quit overthinking.
- [ ] Quit focusing on what you do not have.
- [ ] Quit negative self-talk.
- [ ] Quit making excuses.
- [ ] Quit overexercising.
- [ ] Quit fearing humiliation.
- [ ] Quit going in the popular direction.
- [ ] Quit retreating to your comfort zone.
- [ ] Quit letting others define you.
- [ ] Quit focusing on your setbacks.
- [ ] Quit negative emotions.
- [ ] Quit making your happiness secondary.
- [ ] Quit focusing on yesterday and tomorrow—live in the present.
- [ ] Quit not forgiving others.
- [ ] Quit not forgiving yourself.
- [ ] Quit letting others outhustle you.
- [ ] Quit letting your ego get in the way of your progress.

☐ Quit needing to be in control.
☐ Quit your resistance to change.

Quitting unproductive thoughts, habits, and worry
is just what the doctor ordered.

Feel-Good Story: An Essay by My Daughter

Allie, my daughter, beautiful both inside and out, has suffered from Crohn's disease since she was eight. She wrote this essay when she was seventeen:

Many people perceive failure as a lack of success. What I have learned and experienced firsthand in my life is that perception couldn't be further from the truth. Failing isn't about how many loses one takes or how many setbacks a person encounters. Failing, in my own words, is someone not succeeding and then giving up. The key words are *giving up*. I have dealt with many obstacles in my life, constantly facing defeat yet still persevering to keep moving forward.

When I was eight years old, I was diagnosed with Crohn's disease. It seems this has always been a part of my life. So many activities I have been told I would never be able to do, foods I could not eat. Fortunately I have very optimistic parents who taught me anything can be done. I have grown up with the thought "mind over body" is true and can be achieved. I'm not someone who sits at home and does nothing. I constantly need to be active. Theater is a way for me to express who I am, and it keeps me productive.

I have fought through so many bad times that I believed would never end. My stomach has always been a constant problem that I wished would go away. I asked myself why, why me? The important question is not *why* but, rather, *what*: what can I do to make something good out of this? Find that light at the end of the tunnel. I couldn't see that light until I took a step back from reality and really thought about what Crohn's has done for me—good and bad. It has brought me treacherous moments, yet it has also taught me so many wonderful lessons. I have done things doctors said I would never be able to do.

I have learned that giving up is not an option. Failure is not an option. Yes, there will be days that will be harder than others, but I can't let that get in my way. I get up every day with a smile on my face and work hard when I get to school. I have persevered through rough times and continue to grow as a person. I have stopped asking myself why me and instead started focusing on how this is a good thing.

Oddly enough, it wasn't hard to see just how good my situation is. I wouldn't be who I am today without Crohn's. I'm so much stronger having the experiences I've encountered. I'm wiser and strongheaded. It's not a burden anymore but a challenge. Just like any other challenges, I will find a way through it. Failing is something we all do, but failing and then moving forward is what separates highly successful people from the average person.

I intend to live my life learning and picking myself up as I hurdle over my obstacles. They will get harder as I get older, but I am not the only one who faces difficulties. Everyone has their own setbacks, but it's how we handle them that counts. It's how we see the world and persevere with each roadblock. In the end, I believe failure is only achieved when you give up. If you have the strength and the courage to keep moving forward, win or lose, you have succeeded in your own way. A wise man once told me, "Success is not counted by the number of wins one person has but rather by their strength to find new ways to overcome adversities." Or, as Dory put it, "Just keep swimming."

Remember that each master or expert started off as a novice. A scientist, musician, lawyer, professional athlete, or engineer only achieved what they did because they did not quit. And neither should you! Trust there is a finish line out there with your name on it and don't quit until you get there. And remember as well that everyone who serves as your inspiration is an inspiration because they did not quit.

"Success is not counted by the number of wins
one person has but rather by their strength to find
new ways to overcome adversities."

CHAPTER 4
Your Past Isn't You

If you stare at your past, your future goes flying by.
—BENSON HANSEN

Perhaps this will be the most important chapter you read. Why? Because the advice I've shared so far won't lead you to do anything different if you are carrying your past wounds or regrets like a weight. Are you saddled with the burden of anger, sadness, guilt, fear, anxiety, or disappointment? If so, these emotions will most certainly create self-imposed walls and blockades between you and an enjoyable, happy, fulfilling life.

I am not telling you it's going to be easy to put missteps behind you, but I am telling you it's worth it. You do have time to "edit your life." How do I know this? Truth be told, I was an angry, unhappy young man who had brushes with the law, drank alcohol in excess, got fired from numerous jobs, and, at times, was a menace to society—all before I was twenty.

After high school, I created lots of trouble for myself. I was even convicted of being a "jerk." You heard that right. I got into a bunch of trouble after a crazy night of drinking and fighting and ended up in front of a judge the next day. After he heard the story, he said, "So, you're basically telling me you're a jerk?" He then smacked his gavel to his desk and said, "You're fined $250 for being a jerk!" True story.

These mistakes resulted in low self-esteem, self-doubt, and regret, but I didn't become defeated. I chose to make over my life. Likewise, regret doesn't have to be the end of your story. Your life can have many chapters *if you choose*. It's never too late to be the person you want to be.

It's never too late to be the person you want to be.

Rocky and Me

Even though I was a screwup, one man got through to me and had a big influence on my perspective as a confused, aimless teen. I was just sixteen years old when Sylvester Stallone's *Rocky* hit the theaters. Watching Rocky Balboa beat impossible odds to rise from underdog to bona fide champion opened my eyes to new possibilities. A fire was ignited deep within my heart.

You either let your past control you,
or you decide to control your past.

For me, the transformation wasn't immediate, but a seed was planted. It was then that I began to understand an important concept: even though I wasn't the biggest, strongest, smartest, or most talented guy in the world, I could accomplish just about anything I set my mind to with heart, drive, and determination. Who would have ever thought that, years later, I would be fortunate enough to sit down with Sly Stallone and listen to his insights and wisdom on what it takes to be a winner? His personal success made him a real-life version of Rocky, the iconic role he brought to life on the big screen.

When did I decide to change direction? My time came late one night when I was drinking excessively with a good friend in Greenwich Village, New York. I don't remember the exact block we were on, but it offered at least four bars. As usual, we were doing shots. Back then, Bacardi 151 Rum was my go-to drink. It was high proof, with almost twice the alcohol volume as regular liquor. You could light it on fire just before you swigged it down.

Anyway, I was always up for a good street fight, and, like an idiot, I went bar to bar, fighting the bouncers. By the time it all ended, my shirt was ripped off, and I had plenty of bumps and bruises. You would think that would be enough to stop, but not back in those days. Still a drunken buffoon, I decided to get rough with my friend. I was a respectable kickboxer, so I threw a roundhouse kick to his arm—and almost broke it. I saw his face, and at that moment, I said, "Who the f@#! am I?"

I didn't like the answer, so I said, enough is enough. I was one of the lucky ones. When I decided to stop drinking, it was fairly easy. The person I became when under the influence was, in short, a horror show. My disgust with that version of me was my motivation to quit.

You'll eventually be faced with the same decision I had: either let your past control you or decide to control your past. Don't get sucked into the should-of-could-of game; regret is always the winner in that game. You've made mistakes—so had I. But I chose to change, to leave the mistakes behind and become a better me.

Not a person on the planet can claim to be free of past mistakes. You can live in turmoil, rehashing what you wish you'd done instead. Or, you can look at mistakes as your greatest teachers, the lessons that showed you what you *don't* want to be. Ask yourself this question: what would my life look like if I could move on to the next chapter and leave my mistakes and disappointments in the distant past? I am fairly sure you would breathe a sigh of relief and adopt a more optimistic view of the future.

Let the haunting end. It's time to rearrange your thinking and change your perspective to change your life. You can focus on your past actions or claim a new outlook. A positive attitude doesn't mean ignoring life's troubles. It just means you're looking out for the positive, rather than focusing on the negative. An old mentor of mine use to say, "Being positive doesn't mean you don't have negative thoughts; it just means you don't let them control you."

Psychology Today offers excellent advice on rebounding from the regrets of your past: "It's time to rewrite the story you tell yourself. Don't make the past your present. You can't make yourself forget about the past, but you can choose how often you allow yourself to dwell on it. If you let your past define you, you're limiting yourself both in who you can be and what you can experience in the future. Your life is what is happening to you right now. You, and you alone, have the power to change what this next moment's experience will be by choosing how you respond to painful thoughts, memories, and feelings."[12]

Letter to the Old Me

When you are ready to heal from the past and embrace the potential of the future, it is helpful to write a letter to your old self—a declaration of change and new beginnings. I encourage you to do this exercise today.

While writing, think of the future you; be honest and optimistic. Make it unique to your past experience and your future dreams. Start healing today. I'm providing a sample letter to get you started. Read for inspiration and then get out paper to write your own version.

---

12   Erin Olivo, "How to Put Painful Experiences behind You," *Psychology Today*, September 10, 2015, https://www.psychologytoday.com/us/blog/wise-mind-living/201509/how-put-painful-experiences-behind-you.

Dear Past Me,

I just want to say that I'm glad you're gone. I know that might sound harsh, and please don't take this the wrong way because I am really proud of you. I'm just glad that you seem like a different person to me now. You grew up. You changed. You found yourself again. I hope that you're proud of who you have become because I finally am. I'm glad that I can look at myself and see someone smart, funny, caring, and genuine.

You are independent. You are beautiful. You are worthy. I know you never felt that you were—I remember that feeling. Take each day by stride. Live. Laugh. Love. When it's hard to get up, get up anyway. It's a new day for you to conquer the world and show what you are made of. When everything around you seems to be falling apart, laugh because that's the best type of medicine for those who feel broken—you aren't. When those who try to hurt you do, show them love. Give them the grace that they may not deserve; it may just shock them.

Recently I have learned a lot . . . I learned that things don't always turn out the way you planned, or the way you think they should. And I've learned that there are things that go wrong that don't always get fixed or get put back together the way they were before. I've learned that some broken things stay broken, and I've learned that you can get through bad times and keep looking for better ones, as long as you have people who love you.

I know that in life we do things. Some we wish we had never done. But they all make us who we are. If we were to reverse any of them we wouldn't be the person we are today. So JUST LIVE. Make mistakes. Have wonderful memories.

I am beautifully bruised, scarred, and a much better version of myself. So my friend, I hope you understand I had to let go of a huge part of myself, but that was only to let a better part in. You will be missed, and I will always remember the person I used to be.

But still, good riddance, old me.

Love,

Future Me[13]

Make sure you sign and date your letter, for *this* is the person you are meant to be.

Keep the letter you've written on paper or go to Futureme.org where "you can send your future self words of inspiration or comfort—or maybe a swift kick in the pants."[14]

Don't Let Anybody Define Who You Are

This is a big idea. You will discover people who desperately want to define who you are, what you are, and what you will become. They may even make generalizations and put you in a catch-all category.

Don't let that happen. Don't let anybody define who you are or what you are—except you. One of the best interviews I've had was with Montel Williams, a twenty-two-year military veteran. Montel was the first African American enlisted Marine to complete and graduate from both the Naval Academy Prep School and the US Naval Academy. As a young boy, his teacher said to him, "That is why you people [African Americans] will never get anywhere!" With deep emotion, Montel told me, "I took the sting of that remark and made a promise to myself, that I would be the only person who defines me. Tell your readers: As far as I'm concerned, you need to be your own advocate. You alone have to own the definition of who you are!"

---

13   Emily Ryan Turner, "A Goodbye Letter to the Old Me," *Odyssey*, June 21, 2016, https://www.theodysseyonline.com/goodbye-letter-to-the-old-me.
14   Future Me, https://www.futureme.org.

Don't let the noise of somebody else's negativity or unsupportive opinions drown out your dreams. You have the ability to be great. Through your experiences, develop a set of beliefs, values, and rules to create your own philosophy of life. Embrace your personal gifts and use them as powerful tools. We are all different, so find your own voice and celebrate what makes you special. Don't try to be something you're not. Don't run away from your uniqueness; rather, embrace it, develop it, and take it to the max.

It's fine to learn from others and pick up some of their positive traits, but don't merely imitate somebody else; you will always be in their shadow and second best. Not everybody will understand you or appreciate your unique qualities, and that's okay. You can't please all. Your real friends will not hold you back; they will lift you up and bring out the best in you. As for the naysayers, the best approach is to prove them wrong with the success you will have.

Feel-Good Story: Jimmy Kimmel

The interview I did with comedian, writer, and executive producer Jimmy Kimmel proves my point about rejecting the storylines others try to impose on you. Learn from his example and never let anyone tell you that you are incapable. Early in his career, Jimmy told me he was fired as a radio DJ. He shared his struggles with me:

> The biggest obstacle I have had to overcome in my career is being pigeonholed. And that's not just true in television. It's been true going back to my days when I was on the radio. I remember when I was starting out in radio, there would be certain program directors and general managers who felt I should just be a behind-the-scenes guy or maybe a writer. They felt that I shouldn't be "on-the-air talent." They felt that I would be more suited for a support role to other people who were—in

their minds—more talented. I was even let go from a couple of radio jobs.

I do not want anyone telling me what I am capable or not capable of doing. The best you can do in these situations is to prove the critics wrong.

Life *Does* Have Do-Overs

As long as you have breath, the jury is still out on how you lived your life. What does this mean for you? It is never too late to become the person you were meant to be.

I have a wonderfully optimistic wife whose mantra for us is, "The best is yet to come!" Imagine having that attitude when thinking of your future. That would be incredible, right? Well, you can! Nothing is stopping you from having this hopeful mindset. When you put your past in the past, you are ready for a beautiful, bright future. Will it be the easiest thing you have ever done? No. But forward-looking positivity is essential for unlocking your true potential.

As long as you have breath, the jury is still out
on how you lived your life.

To move on and "do over," look at mistakes as a learning experience. Learn from your past to build a better future. Recognize that missteps and bad decisions are simply part of your journey. My friend Darren Prince wrote the best-selling book *Aiming High,* a memoir of "how a prominent sports and celebrity agent hit bottom at the top." Darren said it best when speaking of the opportunities for do-overs in life: "Whether you're in Yale or in jail, on Park Avenue or a park bench, it's never too late to change your mind about what you want to do with the rest of your life. More importantly, it's never too late to decide what type of person you want to be versus the person you are!"[15]

One of the toughest lessons in life is letting go. Whether it is guilt, anger, love, loss, or betrayal. Change may not be easy, but it is necessary. Aren't you curious how far you could go if you get the past out of your mind? You're stronger, smarter, and more capable than you give yourself credit for. Life is hard enough without letting yourself get dragged down by your past. Move past your past, and then, watch out, world, here you come!

"It's never too late to change your mind about what you want to do with the rest of your life."
—Darren Prince, *Aiming High*

Take Possession of Your Mind

You may consider yourself weak in certain areas, but I guarantee that you'll grow stronger if you banish doubt, regret, and fear from your mind. Take possession of your thoughts and resolve to be fully in control of what you'll dwell on. Then, you'll be ready for your comeback story—a bigger, bolder, more experienced person who has grown in wisdom and prepared for success.

"Emancipate yourselves from mental slavery, none but ourselves can free our minds."
—Bob Marley, "Redemption Song"

---

15 Brandon Steiner, "It's Never Too Late to Be the Person You Want to Be," LinkedIn, November 22, 2018, https://www.linkedin.com/pulse/its-never-too-late-person-you-want-brandon-steiner/.

Think back over your teenage years. Has peer pressure served you well? It's time to distance yourself from negative influences and take possession of your mind. It's time to focus on the small victories and see it's the accumulation of ordinary moments that ultimately determine your life. When would be a good time to take action? Now!

The better you can ride the waves of life, the more you will be able to brush off things that have affected you in the past. *You* are in control of your life. Why? Because your life is no longer controlled by your emotions, and those soul-crushing mistakes made in the past are now a distant memory. You now have a new mindset of self-acceptance. You may not have practiced self-acceptance in the past, but now, you must. Self-acceptance will allow you to forgive yourself and others. Starting today, take possession of your mind and grow in mental fortitude. Then, the person you most admire will be the one looking back at you in the mirror.

Your Toughest Fight

Look no further. Your biggest challenge to change will, no doubt, be you pitted against yourself. You are your toughest because you live with yourself twenty-four hours a day: morning, noon, and night.

Even when you're taking a break from civilization, you're still with you. Your challenge is not the competition, society, your boss, family, or friends. The battle is within you—namely, how you deal with your emotions, handle setbacks, and keep a positive outlook on life. All too often, we blame what we *think* is in our way, when, in truth, the greatest obstacles are self-imposed. Defeating your own bad habits may be the fight of your life.

At times, we could all use an attitude adjustment and perhaps a different code of behavior. Think about how a new attitude might affect your life. Will bringing in more upbeat and optimistic thought patterns and actions result in a happier family, career, or social life? Could it give you a better chance of reaching your goals? If you keep on saying you're "going to do it" but keep waiting for just the right circumstances to fall in place, it will likely never get done. Put excuses aside. It's time to pivot in a new direction.

BJ Neblett, who authored dozens of short stories, poems, and articles, said it well: "We are the sum total of our experiences. Those experiences—be they positive or negative—make us the person we are at any given point in our lives. And, like a flowing river, those same experiences, and those yet to come, continue to influence and reshape the person we are, and the person we become. None of us are the same as we were yesterday, nor will be tomorrow."[16]

Reality is, everybody has a story of doom and gloom. You need to let go of your particular version of "woe is me." As strange as it sounds, perhaps it's been comforting to have your sob story readily available for all to hear. Maybe you have been using your sad history to elicit pity or as an excuse for why you're not where you want to be in life. Ask yourself, has holding on to the past served you well? Or has it led to becoming self-absorbed and stuck? The truth is, it has likely trapped you and held you back from reaching your true full potential.

You are your toughest opponent because you live with yourself twenty-four hours a day: morning, noon, and night.

Many are familiar with the 12 Steps of Alcoholics Anonymous, which outline a proven strategy for personal change and growth. Let's borrow their first two steps as we begin our journey toward a better

---

16   B.J. Neblett Quotes, Goodreads, https://www.goodreads.com/quotes/1222185-we-are-the-sum-total-of-our-experiences-those-experiences.

you.[17] The first step in true self-discovery is to be honest with yourself. I am not talking about self-criticism. I am talking about a productive process of learning who you are; I'm suggesting a courageous inventory of strengths and weakness, talents and struggles. Only then can you envision a winning future tailor made for you. Only then can you reinvent your outlook and attitude to write a brighter, more promising, and achievable next chapter.

The next step is to reflect on any amends you want to make. Do you need to apologize or clean up a mess before moving on? Let's get it done. Apologies are often necessary to diffuse harsh emotions, resolve conflicts, and neutralize resentment. A vulnerable mea culpa can help everyone in the healing process. It may be hard to take responsibility for your part in an incident, but it's necessary if you want to move forward with a clean slate.

In most cases, you will look at the past through your own lens while others will have a different perspective. Remember, the goal is to put past negativity behind you. So, be the bigger person and step forward first. Be less concerned with setting the record straight than making things right. The sooner you become accountable for your part in the matter—no matter how small you think it is—the sooner you can move forward. Be careful not to emphasize your side of the story. No one wants a conditional, half-hearted apology. I have found writing a letter can work well. It adds a personal touch of sincerity and gives time for the other party to digest your words before reacting. It also gives you the opportunity to edit your words—something that's impossible in person.

Next, give yourself a break. Self-forgiveness is crucial. We are all human, which means we all make mistakes. Carrying guilt, shame, and self-hatred will only lead to low self-esteem, self-doubt, pain, and

---

17 Nicole Monaco and Scot Thomas, "Alcoholics Anonymous (AA) & the 12 Steps," Alcohol.org, July 14, 2019, https://www.alcohol.org/alcoholics-anonymous/.

heartache—not a good recipe for a happy life. If others are not receptive to your apology, you still need to move on. Perhaps, in the future, the time will be right to set things straight, but until then, do not carry the anxiety and mental stress indefinitely.

The best way to prove you have changed is to change for all to see. Work on building up your self-worth. I like to describe self-worth as an animal that needs to be fed; many things can feed that animal, like helping and giving to others, reaching your goals, practicing gratitude, doing the right thing, and (a favorite of mine) physical fitness. It's not about solving all the world's problems; it's about looking around and noticing where you can be of help and service. Open your eyes, and you may see many opportunities where your assistance can have dramatic, positive changes on individuals. In turn, you will feel better about yourself.

Self-worth is an animal that needs to be fed.

Let me tell you about Calvin Cordozar Broadus Jr., better known as Snoop Dog. I met and interviewed Snoop for my first book. He was the high school class clown and also an alleged gang member in the infamous Rollin' 20 Crips on the east side of Long Beach, California. Snoop had numerous brushes with the law. In an interview he did for *The Howard Stern Show*, he said, "Growing up in the environment I came from, I am not proud of all I did. But it was a learning experience. My role models and mentors used to be drug dealers and gangsters. Now I am feeding off positive energy. Going to jail showed me a place that I did not want to be." Reflecting on the past, he said, "Sometimes a loss is the best thing that can happen. It can teach you what you should have done—and what you should do next time." So what's the moral of the story? Don't let your past dictate your future.

Put your ego aside. The victory you seek is within, but don't be afraid to ask for guidance. Look for a role model or a professional to help your efforts. We all have a history, so speak with your elders; they will have plenty of useful suggestions from their history.

Whatever it takes to put your past behind you, get it done. Start saying no to things that are not productive for you. Put the necessary boundaries in place. All this needs to happen guilt free. Seek out and hang out with positive people. Surround yourself with optimism. Stop feeding on negativity.

You have a choice throughout the day. As your coach, I am telling you to run away from depressing situations. Run to joy and happiness instead. And if you're going to focus on the past, focus on your *positive* past, the times you were the best version of yourself. And don't tell me you don't have any positive memories. We all do—including you!

Here are two quick stories from highly successful people I have interviewed or done business with that will help make my point. Notice how they turned past negative situations into ammunition for their ambitions.

Five-time Grammy nominee and rap artist Kid Rock was a self-admitted drug dealer and had a son he didn't know about. What he thought would be horrible turned out to be a blessing:

> See, back when I was still pretty much a kid myself, my son basically showed up on my doorstep when he was six years old. The truth of the matter is that you don't have a lot of choices at a point like that. Sometimes life makes choices for you, and your choice is in how well you handle it. You've got to be careful what you consider an obstacle in your life. What I once thought could be the biggest obstacle in my life turned out to be the greatest thing that ever happened to me and one of my biggest lessons. I worried that it was going to screw up my life, but it became the most educational and important thing!

Don't let anyone lock you up with your past issues.
Liberate yourself.

One of my favorite interviews was with Evander "The Real Deal" Holyfield. He turned around racism, self-doubt, and training mistakes to become an Olympian and five-time World Heavyweight Boxing Champion:

As a young kid, I came from a very negative world; most would consider where I grew up as the ghetto. I didn't learn how to read and felt very bad about myself. I was very insecure. I never understood why I couldn't read. When I was young, I really didn't enjoy boxing. I could barely get through a three-round fight because I was fighting in the South, and I was rarely given a fair shot at a decision. I let that get to me, and so I didn't pace myself. I just went out there trying to hit as hard as I could, and I often lost my stamina early. When I got older, I was able to travel. I found the fights were judged more fairly, so I learned to pace myself. I learned the importance of relaxing in the ring. I learned early on that life is a constant test. As I've grown older, I have learned that if you love something, you can be successful. Many things along the way won't work out, but if you love what you're doing, you can overcome all. In life you can learn anything—you may not be the best, but you can learn. I've always been open to listening to others, following directions, and making sure I did not quit. My philosophy is don't let someone else steal your joy. Even if you don't get the decision, keep the victory!

Become proactive: *that* will win the game. Don't go wide and shallow in your relationships; instead, go narrow and deep. Don't let anyone lock you up with your past issues. Liberate yourself from negative people. They are toxic; they are not there to help you but to bring you down.

Trust is the hardest thing to earn and the easiest thing to lose. Always remember "relationship capital" is just as important as money capital. Work on this each day. The opportunity train is leaving, so get on it! A great life is one on your terms. Let the future guide you, not the past.

CHAPTER 5

Setting Your Goals: Milestones and Objectives

The Time for Thinking Is Over

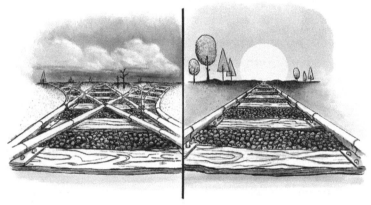

Over Thinking
Destroys Goals

Focused Mind-Set
To Achieve

rifting without aim or a sense of purpose is off the table. Setting specific, actionable goals will help you stay focused and motivated. Your mind is a powerful resource you can use to create the life that you desire. Tom Terwilliger, my childhood friend, is equal parts athlete, entrepreneur, and motivator. Five years after pulling himself from the world of drug and alcohol addiction, Tom's never-give-up attitude, determination, and willingness to sweat earned him a National Body Building Championship (Mr. America) title and a successful sixteen-year career as a Fox Sports Net show host. Tom is also the author of the best-selling book *7 Rules of Achievement*. He learned the importance of setting goals when he determined to turn his life around: "I knew how to set goals and accomplish what I wanted. I wanted to become an outlaw biker, and I became one. Then I turned my attention to becoming Mr. America, and in 1986, that's what I became."

Goal setting gives meaning to your life. You have hope and excitement as you take fate into your hands. Your future life is not what you do some of the time; it's what you do correctly and consistently. A well-thought-out plan will bring structure to your daily activities and turn past difficulty and struggle into stepping-stones. A boost in your confidence and self-worth will be one of many benefits.

Will you be challenged? Yes, but keep in mind, you are not preordained to be a success or a failure, and neither failure nor success is an overnight event. It's about a lifestyle, about adopting a good attitude and productive habits. Formulating and following through with your goal one step at a time is the most effective way to reach the finish line.

Does the previous paragraph sound a bit familiar? Most likely yes. Others have likely told you to be persistent and consistent, but few really understand the mechanics of why most goals go unrealized. Many topics are covered in this book but few will be more important than understanding the productive goal setting. I will make this as simple as possible.

You have a goal, so you start thinking and planning. The beginning of the process is the time for pragmatic thought, for envisioning the necessary steps to achieve your ambitions. Do not rush this stage. If done correctly, you will seek out the best advice and do your due diligence. Be circumspect and put a sound course of action in place.

Once you have a clear, concise strategy, turn off your thinking brain. Have you ever come up short of a goal? Perhaps you began all gung ho but then gave up. Why? You were guilty of overthinking. Perhaps you listened to others who pointed out the difficulties you might face. A little voice in your head compiled a list of reasons why you would fail. This lead to pondering, which led to procrastination. And then, you quit. Halting this process of overthinking, of overanalyzing, is what separates those who achieve their goals from those who do not.

Once you have a clear, concise strategy, turn off your thinking brain . . . move forward, under any and all conditions.

Moral of the story: compose your game plan and then set out to achieve it. Put thinking aside and move forward, under any and all conditions. Trust the process. Don't worry about the future or the past. Adjust when necessary. Be proactive and take action with each step of the plan. Do this, and your pathway to great achievement will be clear.

Manage Your Time

You want to have a big advantage over the competition, right? So, how about giving yourself a big head start? Let's face it. We each have twenty-four hours in a day, so we need to use them wisely. I am one of the lucky ones; early in my twenties, I adopted a solid set of rules to impose structure on my day. I read self-help books and noticed an overlapping theme: bring structure into your life for success. I believed it and put it into action.

Back then, I started a business, earned a black belt in karate, ran marathons, travelled often from New York to California, and still had plenty of time for partying and socializing. Fast-forward. Now I'm in my late fifties. I run a couple of businesses, study jujitsu, and roll with guys half my age. I rehabbed my back from two back surgeries, am happily married, and have raised three wonderful children. I take time for vacations, write books, and as my wife will tell you, I still get eight hours of sleep each night. I'm definitely not the night owl I used to be.

I tell you this not to brag but to convince you that implementing structure into your day can have big payoffs. You can take care of the things you need to do for success and still have time for what you enjoy. Without structure and a game plan, I would have been lost. I would not be enjoying the full, rich life I now wake up to each day. I couldn't be more thankful to have learned the importance of structure and time optimization in my twenties.

Like most things in life, you either manage your schedule or your schedule will manage you. If you're overwhelmed by all that needs to get done, it will "melt your brain." You will be depressed and wonder why others get so much done but you can't.

You may think you don't need structure in your life but you're wrong. In the past, perhaps you let your emotions overwhelm logic. This needs to stop. Structure is a great way of organizing your life so that you truly understand the direction you are going and are no longer cast about according to your ever-changing mood. You will wake up with a sense of ownership, order, and organization. You won't be guessing what needs to be done; you will have your priorities all set. A new you will emerge, one that is more productive and less stressed. You'll be refreshed and ready to enjoy life.

So, how can you get going? How can you organize your life for optimization? Let me share some helpful hints. If you have a significant other, bring them into the project. This is not about increasing stress; it's about reducing your stress. So, discuss the changes you envision with the important people who surround you. Often collaboration yields the best results.

Another helpful hint is to recognize the importance of attention. If you want to be a high achiever, you must be "all in" when working on something. Your mind can't be in other places; you need focus, giving your full attention to one task at a time. I visualize all the things I need to do and place each task in a "box." For example, I have a family box, exercise box, relaxation box, writing box, work box, etc. Each box is distinct from the other. When I am ready to work on a box, I take it off my "mental shelf" and I give it 110 percent commitment. I picture myself working within that one box before taking another box down. This exercise allows me to concentrate on the task at hand with no interruptions.

Let's talk about your to-do list. The single-most important daily activity I do that leads to achieving my goals is managing and updating my to-do list. Does this surprise you? It shouldn't. Without an intentional, prioritized list of items to accomplish, you waste time drifting. A subtle form of procrastination is doing lesser-order tasks while ignoring the harder but more essential tasks. Have you ever cleaned the garage to avoid that crucial but difficult email you needed to send? An updated, specific to-do list keeps you accountable.

How long does it take to write or update a to-do list? Maybe five minutes a day. I recommend doing this first thing in the morning before you open emails or check your social media. Set your agenda and envision the day's goals before you become distracted. You'll have greater chances of staying focused if you prioritize your must-dos daily.

We can spend more time thinking of what needs to get done than actually doing it.

You'll find this to-do list tip in many self-development books. Why? Because it works. If you're like me, you probably have a very active mind. Often in the middle of the night, a thought comes to me. Instead of trying to remember it—which produces stress that hinders sleep—I simply write it down or use a voice recorder. After this, my mind is at ease because I have a system in place for capturing these thoughts, and I know I can trust the system. The idea will be there for me in the morning when I'm ready to update my list.

My to-do list has evolved. Thirty years ago, I used scraps of paper; then, I kept a dedicated yellow note pad with me. When I went into business, I bought a nice leather folder that I still have. Chances are, my tattered old folder is older than most readers of this book! You millennials may be more comfortable keeping your lists on mobile devices.

Back in the day, I kept a list of what needed to be done for my company. When I got married, the list grew as I added household chores and responsibilities. When my wife and I had children, the list expanded again.

When I started studying Brazilian jujitsu, believe me, I had to have my to-do list of what I needed to practice. If not, when I went to the dojo, more often than not, I would have been smashed. These days, I use less paper and more audio and video. I keep folders in my phone of what and when something needs to be done. I could in no way handle all the many things I juggle—both in business and personally—without my daily to-do list.

What are some other good reasons to keep an up-to-date to-do list? Your productivity will increase as your stress decreases. You'll more easily gain a sense of accomplishment and will feel at peace, knowing you have it all under control. If you are not sure what belongs on that list, seek out others who have "been there, done that," those with experience and knowledge in your chosen field.

Set a Deadline

When younger, I was no stranger to procrastination. If I had a must-do deadline, in business or my personal life, the hours before the deadline were a mad dash to make sure all was done. I recall being only a couple of days away from an extended overseas trip. In just a few hours, items that had been sitting on my desk for weeks got done. I was suddenly, magically motivated. It's amazing how much you can get done when a deadline is fast approaching. Now, even if I don't have a formal deadline, I assign myself deadlines on most things I do. For me—and perhaps for you too—setting a due date is a handy psychological trick to ensure that all will be done in a timely manner.

If a task takes less than three minutes, don't bother putting it on your to-do list. Get it done immediately when you think of it. It's amazing how we can spend more time thinking of what needs to get done than actually doing it.

While speaking of productivity, let's consider how often you should check in with your smartphone. I check my business email throughout the day but stay away from social media during work hours. The marketing company Mediakix calculated average time spent per day on YouTube (forty minutes), Facebook (thirty-five), Snapchat (twenty-five), Instagram (fifteen), and Twitter (one).[18] If those figures are projected over a lifetime, an alarming number results: five years and four months spent on social media. If these platforms are not moving you closer to your goals, don't waste your time looking at what others are doing. Get busy doing what *you're* supposed to be doing.

Reward yourself with a quick scroll whenever you hit an important milestone or achieve a specific goal. But don't let your reward hinder your long-term objectives. Camping out on social media can go beyond mere distraction to numb you to the life happening around you or may even increase anxiety or depressive symptoms—obstacles to the full, dynamic life we're after.

---

18   "How Much Time Do We Spend on Social Media?," MediaKix, December 16, 2016, https://mediakix.com/blog/how-much-time-is-spent-on-social-media-lifetime/.

Remember your ultimate goals. Add to/edit your to-do list accordingly. If items can be delegated to others, by all means do it. I enjoy writing books, but spelling and grammar aren't a strength for me. My solution is to hire an editor to help me get from concept to completion.

On your journey, be prepared for curveballs. Plans don't always work exactly as we'd like. We all like a clear beginning and a clean, direct ending, but that is just not reality. When your plans go awry, it is important to stay strong and ask yourself, what is the next task at hand? But don't let setbacks unnerve you. Expect them. One step forward and two steps back is something that highly successful people deal with all the time. What separates them from the average person is that they keep moving forward, never losing sight of the final outcome.

Make a Commitment to Yourself in Writing

Bruce Lee, world-renowned martial artist, actor, philosopher, and father of two, wrote himself a letter at the age of twenty-nine, setting out the personal goals he had for his future. He titled the letter "My Definite Chief Aim" and used it as a constant reminder to stay focused on his goals. Three years after setting these specific goals, he met and surpassed what he set out to achieve:

I, Bruce Lee, will be the first highest paid Oriental super star in the United States. In return I will give the most exciting performances and render the best of quality in the capacity of an actor. Starting 1970 I will achieve world fame and from then onward till the end of 1980 I will have in my possession $10,000,000. I will live the way I please and achieve inner harmony and happiness.

Bruce Lee, January 1969[19]

Use Smart Goals

I've set and reached many goals by going on autopilot, putting my nose to the grindstone, and persevering until the end. However, when trying to explain my process to friends and family, I lacked detail and came up short in the way I communicated. But shortly after my first book, I took an intensive year-long life-coaching course, which gave me a systematized, easy-to-understand, and comprehensive approach to setting and reaching goals: SMART goals.

The first-known use of the term "SMART goals" occurred in the November 1981 issue of *Management Review* by George T. Doran.[20] SMART is an anacronym to help you remember the steps to successful goal setting. I've adjusted some of the original content to make this concept work for me specifically. I think you, too, could benefit from this approach.

Specific: Target a specific area for improvement. Vague goals get you nowhere fast, so be as specific as you can about your desired outcome. To say I want to be rich or I want to get a great job is not helpful. Zoom in and put a spotlight on the distinct end result you seek.

Measurable: Look for progress. Can you measure that you are closer to your goal than you were yesterday, last week, or last month? In other words, can you mark clear progress? The journey will have ups and downs. An objective method to measure overall progress will keep you from catastrophizing during the downs. You can stay positive and

---

19 "My Definite Chief Aim," Letters of Note, March 16, 2011, http://www.lettersofnote.com/2011/03/my-definite-chief-aim.html.

20 George T. Doran, "There's a S.M.A.R.T. Way to Write Management Goals and Objectives," *Management Review* (November 1981), https://community.mis.temple.edu/mis0855002fall2015/files/2015/10/S.M.A.R.T-Way-Management-Review.pdf.

give yourself proper credit as you measure forward movement—even if in small increments.

Attainable: Don't bite off more than you can chew: It's fine to think big and aim high or stretch yourself to see how far you can really go, but you must still make the goal realistic and within your reach. Start with small, achievable goals. Then, before you know it, you'll be climbing a mountain, one step at a time. You'll have the satisfaction of looking to see how far you have gone. If you set a goal that is too lofty, you will likely talk yourself out of it before you even begin.

Relevant: Choose an important goal, one directly related to your priorities and ultimate purpose. If the goal seems tangential or untrue to you, you will lack the drive to finish.

Time-related: Specify when the result will be achieved by constructing a timeline for your goal. Then, stick with it as best you can, allowing for the truly unforeseen. A nonspecific timetable will be ammunition for delay and procrastination. One of my strategies for reaching goals is to promise myself a fixed deadline. When I say I'm going to do something, I allow no ifs, ands, or buts. I do it. That determined drive to do is part of my personality. The last thing I want to do is disappoint others. This helps me maintain laser focus on the task at hand.

SMART Goals Template

(Adapted from zestwellness.squarespace.com › SMART-Goals-template.)

SMART goals are designed to help you identify if what you want to achieve is realistic and then to set a deadline. When writing SMART goals, use concise language but include relevant information. These goals are designed to help you succeed, so write with clarity and stay focused and upbeat.

Initial Goal *(Write the goal you have in mind.)*

_____

_____

_____

_____

_____

_____

_____

1. Specific *(What specifically do you want to accomplish?)*

_____

_____

_____

_____

_____

_____

2. Measurable *(How can you measure intermediate progress and know if you are getting closer to your goal?)*

_____

_____

_____

_____

_____

_____

3. Achievable *(Do you have the skills and resources required to achieve the goal? If not, can you obtain them? How?)*

_____

_____

_____

_____

_____

_____

_____

4. Relevant *(What is your motivation for this goal? What are the positive emotions you hope to feel upon completion of the goal? How will you step out of your comfort zone to achieve this goal?)*

_____

_____

_____

_____

_____

_____

_____

5. Time-bound *(What's the deadline, and is it realistic?)*
*You can make minigoals with deadlines to keep you motivated.

_____

_____

_____

_____

_____

_____

_____

SMART Goal *(Review what you have written and craft a new goal statement based on your answers to the questions above.)*

_____

_____

_____

_____

_____

_____

_____

Signature:

Date:

Visual Aids

Have you heard of the VARK model of learning styles? According to this theory, individuals have one primary medium for taking in information most effectively, either visual, auditory, reading/writing, or kinesthetic. Do you prefer one of these forms over the others when learning something new? Now, consider what clinical psychologist Haig Kouyoumdjian, PhD, has to say about visual learning specifically:

A large body of research indicates that visual cues help us to better retrieve and remember information. The research outcomes on visual learning make complete sense when you consider that our brain is mainly an image processor (much of our sensory cortex is devoted to vision), not a word processor.

In fact, the part of the brain used to process words is quite small in comparison to the part that processes visual images.[21]

Wow. So, according to Kouyoumdjian's comment, we'd be foolish only to use a written to-do list to propel us forward. Would you agree that visuals can be effective learning or memory tools? This could include photos, illustrations, icons, symbols, sketches, figures, and concept maps, to name only a few. After all, it's commonly said that a picture is worth a thousand words.

Use an hourglass to visualize life's moments. Each grain of sand falls, and once it's down, the sand can never go back up.

Dan Caldwell, AKA "Punkass," is a good friend of mine. He's also president of the apparel company TapouT. He and his two friends, Charles "Mask" Lewis and Tim "Skyskrape" Katz, founded TapouT, generally recognized as the first brand to represent the sport of Mixed Martial Arts (MMA). They started selling T-shirts out of the trunk of their car, and years later, they sold the company for more than $200 million. Dan uses visual aids as part of his success strategy:

I always let myself know, as soon as I am attacking a new goal, that there is no Plan B. Once I start traveling down that path, nothing can stop me! I close all my doors of escape, and I will fight to the death. Rejecting the idea of a Plan B helps you adopt a sense of urgency too. In 1519, Hernán Cortés faced

---

21 Haig Kouyoumdjian PhD, "Learning through Visuals," *Psychology Today* blog, July 20, 2012, https://www.psychologytoday.com/us/blog/get-psyched/201207/learning-through-visuals.

overwhelming odds when he landed in Mexico with only five hundred soldiers on his eleven ships. He knew he was going to face an Aztec army of over five hundred thousand men. Aware of his desperate circumstances, he ordered that all the ships be burned! Giving his small army no way to retreat, he demanded, "Victory, or death with honor!" Those soldiers fought and were victorious in part because there was no Plan B. I eliminated my Plan B with my tattoos. I don't tell anyone to get tattoos, but it was something that worked for me. The tattoos on my hands and neck represent that I can never again go back to a nine-to-five job. That was my burning-the-ships moment! Today I carry a two-hundred-year-old Spanish coin wherever I go. It bears the image of Hernán Cortés, and, along with those tattoos, it reminds me that I have no Plan B. I must make it!

Another good friend and ultrasuccessful associate of mine uses an hourglass to visualize his entire life. He watches each grain of sand fall, and once down, the sand can never go back up. To him it means each second, minute, and hour of the day is precious.

In his office, he has an actual hourglass. On his smartphone, his wallpaper is an image of the same. It sounds simple, but for him, this visual aid is a constant reminder that he has no time for shortcuts or excuses.

What visual aid might you use to remind you of the importance of your goal?

Pushing through Pain to the Very End

In the movie *The Equalizer 2*, Denzel Washington's character says, "There's two kinds of pain in this world: pain that hurts and pain that alters."

Reaching your goals requires an understanding of pain, and pain comes in many forms. It can be physical or emotional pain, the pain of rejection, the pain of not being where you want to be in life, or even the pain of being out of your comfort zone. The manner in which your mind handles pain will determine how quickly and effectively you reach goals. The ability to shift the pain from something you flee to something you use as a stepping-stone, teachable moment, or motivating force is one of the keys to your success.

You will not get to the place you want to be if you do not embrace and endure the pain required to pursue your dream. A strong mindset is a must if you plan to "go for the gold." Drive and desire must trump the pain that may come when striving for achievement. The anxiety of getting out of your comfort zone must be less than the anxiety of not being where you want to be. You will most likely experience plenty of painful rejection as you pursue your goals—a lot of nos for each yes. Expect that pain; understand it; accept it; and grow as an individual from it.

"There's two kinds of pain in this world: pain that hurts
and pain that alters."
—The Equalizer 2

Often, you do not have control over your circumstances. Therefore, you cannot let your circumstances define you. My old football coach used to say, "If you get knocked down, get back up and dust yourself off." When life knocks you off course, get back up. With each painful misstep, you gain wisdom and experience. It's okay if you come out of it with a battle scar or two. That's to be expected. You will prosper in the long run if you adopt the mindset of "dusting yourself off" and continuing to take one step after another.

You have the ability to be great at something. In fact, I would bet that you can think back to a moment in time when you were at your best. And I am sure you'd agree that, in that moment, your mindset played a significant role. You likely exhibited endless confidence and self-discipline and didn't let outside influences or self-doubt get in your way. The momentum of an empowered mindset can rocket you toward your goals. As you move forward, prepare your mind and get ready for the pain that might come.

Reaching your goals and achieving success doesn't occur by accident. Don't fall into the trap of thinking somebody will come knocking at your door to hand you instant success. Any great achiever will tell you that it's an arduous trip to the top. And you can count on your competition getting up early and staying up late. Don't let them pass you as they do the things you aren't willing to do. Get tough. Remember, no Plan B. Subscribe to the concept that success takes intense dedication and a consistently strong mindset. Visualize a finish line out there with your name and goal on it and don't stop pressing forward until you plow through it.

Behind the biggest success stories are the people who have outdone and outlasted their competitors. Don't leave anything to chance or luck. Take steps to solve problems that others haven't; have the "stick-to-it" attitude—even during seasons of trial and adversity. Self-pity, helplessness, and a victim mentality have no place. Look at setbacks and mistakes as mere bumps in the road—*not* as a reflection of your true potential.

The Ulysses Contract

Have you ever heard of a Ulysses pact or Ulysses contract? A Ulysses contract is a "freely made decision that is designed and intended to bind oneself in the future."[22] In other words, it's a promise to yourself that

---

22   Bryan Braun, "The Ulysses Contract," November 11, 2012, https://www. bryanbraun.com/2012/11/11/ulysses-contract/.

can really stick. Answer the questions below and keep this exercise as a reminder when you are fatigued, experience self-doubt, or suffer setbacks.

MY ULYSSES CONTRACT: WHEN THE GOING GETS TOUGH

Why am I on this mission?

_____

_____

_____

_____

_____

_____

_____

Under what circumstances did I determine to take on this goal?

_____

_____

_____

_____

_____

_____

_____

How will I feel if I give up?

_____

_____

_____

_____

_____

_____

Who would I be letting down if I gave up?

_____

_____

_____

_____

_____

_____

How will I keep myself inspired? What or who will be my positive forces?

_____

_____

_____

_____

_____

_____

When I am overwhelmed, what will I do to give myself a break?

_____

_____

_____

_____

_____

Will I make excuses, or will I find solutions during difficult times? Explain.

_____

_____

_____

_____

_____

_____

In five years, will I be proud of myself if I accomplished this goal?

_____

_____

_____

_____

_____

_____

What will be my big emotional reward once I accomplish this goal?

_____

_____

_____

_____

_____

When the going gets tough, am I going to "get going," or will I bow my head in defeat?

_____

_____

_____

_____

_____

Signature:

Date:

Subscribe to the concept that success takes intense dedication
and a consistently strong mindset.

Rule Number One and Other Tips

Put in place a rock-solid, powerful support team. Whether it's one person or several, mentors can keep you excited and help you make adjustments or adopt new strategies along the way. Don't say you don't know anybody who could fill this role. Put effort into locating a qualified mentor for support. Successful people enjoy the emotional reward of helping you succeed, so don't be afraid to ask. Getting the right support in place can make all the difference in the world. You need both encouragement and accountability, so that could mean having more than one mentor walking alongside you.

Don't be driven to be perfect; be driven to implement your plan. "Front load" or, in other words, start with the task(s) you don't want to do. Get the necessary but tedious or mundane projects out of the way. Your load will feel lighter. Don't waste your time comparing yourself to others—have your own standards and apply yourself to the work that's yours to do.

And, finally, don't forget about Rule Number One: Push self-doubt aside. Take massive, proactive, well-thought-out, consistent action to create the life you desire. Be focused, eliminate distractions. Being single-minded and determined is the way to see your goal through, from thought to reality.

Prepare Like a Warrior

I had the privilege of publishing the first mixed martial arts (MMA) fine art line, featuring many of the top Ultimate Fighting Championship (UFC) fighters in the world. I was honored to work with many world champions, including Anderson "The Spider" Silva, Chuck Liddell, and two-division champion Georges St-Pierre, who is widely regarded as one of the greatest fighters in UFC history. In his book, *The Way of the Fight*, Georges describes his journey from being bullied as a kid to becoming one of the greatest champions in UFC history. Concerning his method of preparing for fights, he writes, "I want to fight guys who are better than me in all kinds of techniques. I want my training to be harder than my actual fights so I can be prepared to face my toughest opponents—so I can be ready to deal with fear."

"For every two minutes of glamour, there are eight hours of hard work."
—Reporter Jessica Savitch

Or how about the fighting elite, the Navy Seals? Their slogan is, "The more you sweat in peacetime, the less you bleed in war." Warrior-like preparation sets the stage for success. High achievers understand that the success and satisfaction they get from preparing for competition enables them to stay mentally stronger just a little bit longer than their competitors, which can often be the difference between winning and losing. A victor is born when skills, preparation, and even the sweat and tears of endurance all come together. This applies not only to an athlete or business executive but also to the student studying for exams or the mom striving to raise a family.

Use the Science of Deliberate Practice to Dominate

Remember our goal here is for you to become the best you can be, leaving nothing to chance or luck. If you are looking to outperform others using scientific facts and research, then read on for the findings of Swedish psychologist K. Anders Ericsson, a professor at Florida State

University. He has done a great deal of work pertaining to success and is recognized as one of the world's leading researchers on expertise. His studies show that high-level success is not a birthright. *The Cambridge Handbook of Expertise and Expert Performance*, written by Ericsson and his colleagues, is the first handbook where the world's foremost experts on expertise review the scientific knowledge on expert performance and how experts differ from nonexperts. In the book, he explains that extraordinary chess players, business leaders, and athletes have what he calls, "Deliberate, well-structured practice."

I have highlighted key phrases from this book for you to consider as you strive for your personal high level of performance. My suggestion is that you read this several times to capture and take in a full understanding [italics mine]:

Deliberate, well-structured practice is *focused*, programmatic, carried out *over extended periods of time,* guided by conscious performance monitoring, evaluated by *analyses of errors* and procedures *directed at eliminating error. Specific goals* are set at successive stages of expertise development. It involves appropriate, immediate *feedback about performance.* The feedback can be obtained by objective observers—human teachers or coaches—or can be self-generated by *comparing one's own performance with examples of more advanced expert performance.* Such objective feedback helps the learner of expertise to internalize how to identify and correct errors, to set new goals, to *focus on overcoming weakness,* and to monitor progress. Deliberate and well-structured practice builds on setting goals that *go beyond one's current level* of performance and thus *may lead to failures* or even lower performance.

Aspiring expert performers come to view failures as opportunities to improve.[23]

Four Key Takeaways

a. Be focused and pragmatic.

b. Have specific goals that go beyond your current level.

c. Be willing to improve through repetition and be willing to learn from setbacks.

d. In order to advance, have an expert observe, monitor, analyze, and comment.

DELIBERATE PRACTICE WORKSHEET

Use this worksheet to set goals and obtain feedback in a more deliberate, structured manner.

a. What is your *specific, attainable* goal that goes beyond your current level?

b. _____

_____

_____

_____

_____

_____

---

23 K. Anders Ericsson, Neil Charness, Paul J. Feltovich, and Robert R. Hoffman, eds., *The Cambridge Handbook of Expertise and Expert Performance* (Cambridge: Cambridge Univ Press, 2006).

c. How will you stay focused? How will you establish and maintain a will-to-win mindset, even during setbacks?

d. _____

_____

_____

_____

_____

_____

e. What is your daily, weekly, and monthly time commitment to learning and practicing as you become an expert in your chosen field?

f. _____

_____

_____

_____

_____

_____

g. Who is qualified and willing to observe and offer expert analysis and feedback on how you can improve? Before you say, "I don't have anybody," really stop and think. Many people who have achieved success also enjoy helping others. Consider researching experts online to find someone who can examine your work and help you incorporate best practices into your efforts.

h. _____

_____

_____

_____

_____

_____

Signature:

Date:

Best Practices

Closely related to deliberate practice, "best practice" should become your new favorite term. "A best practice is a method or technique that has been generally accepted as superior to any alternatives because it produces results that are superior to those achieved by other means or because it has become a standard way of doing things."[24] Imagine a road map of what has worked well in the past. A best practice is a superior way of accomplishing your goals when compared to other ways.

How do you find best practices? Google the words you have interest in for your specific goal (e.g., making money, overcoming stress, how to sleep). Then follow your query with the words "best practices." You will find an abundance of relevant information and strategies to help you pursue your dreams and ambitions.

Newton's "Laws of Motivation"

As a mentor, I'm always looking for new ways to help others reframe their current thinking. I want them to have an "aha" moment, a moment of sudden realization, inspiration, insight, or comprehension that brings clarity. Paul Tatasciore, a friend and Brazilian jujitsu brother,

---

24 "Best Practice," *Wikipedia* page, last updated June 14, 2019, https://en.wikipedia. org/wiki/Best_practice.

holds degrees both in physics and philosophy. He currently is pursuing a PhD in physics. I asked Paul to explore the idea that somehow the laws of physics could be connected to self-development.[25] I love what Paul came back with.

Because physics is the study of nature and humans are part of nature, we are no exception to the laws of physics. We are governed by these laws and perhaps by some that are yet unknown. Arguably the most fundamental of the laws of physics are Isaac Newton's three laws of motion, which describe the relationship between bodies, forces, and motion. By drawing connections to self-development, maybe these laws can provide insight into how to direct our daily lives.

Newton's Laws

1. An object either remains at rest or continues to move at a constant velocity, unless acted upon by a force.

Picture a rock traveling in the vast emptiness of space. Without any forces acting on it, this rock will move at a constant speed in the same direction, perhaps headed toward nothing of importance. Now instead, picture a rocket ship that can change its velocity and force itself toward any direction the pilot chooses. I invite you to ask yourself, *Which would I rather be: a stagnant rock or a self-directed rocket ship?* If we want to take control of our speed and direction in life, we should strive to be like the rocket ship. According to Newton's first law, in order to change our direction of motion—or perhaps the direction of our lives—we need to, much like the rocket ship, push ourselves to do so.

---

25   Newton's Laws of Motion, National Aeronautics and Space Administration, https://www.grc.nasa.gov/www/k-12/airplane/newton.html.

2. Force is equal to the change in momentum over time (sometimes stated as force equals mass times acceleration).

In other words, the more we, the rocket ship, force ourselves, the more we can change our momentum and accelerate toward the desired destination. We may need to do this while other forces are at play. Several external bodies—whether planets and stars or coworkers and competitors or even family and friends—pull us in opposing directions. But if we strive to be the rocket ship, we can go where we choose. The rock, however, does not possess this ability. The rock is bound to the same path and only changes direction based on the forces provided by its surroundings. We are always better off controlling our own destiny rather than waiting for circumstances to change.

3. For every action there is an equal and opposite reaction.

The rocket ship propels itself by making use of Newton's third law. In order to go forward, it burns fuel. The fuel expands and causes the rocket to push back on the exhaust gas, thereby creating a force in the desired direction. In order to create a force to push us forward in life, perhaps we can learn from this analogy. Look for fuel: past experiences, undesired emotions, negative feelings, etc. Push back on them, against them, to launch yourself forward.

What's the takeaway? We should strive to be like rocket ships, self-propelled and self-directed, as opposed to stagnant space rocks, which are constrained by outside forces (perhaps self-imposed limits or bad habits). A rocket ship can force itself toward a desired destination rather than staying on a constant path to nowhere. The more we force ourselves, the faster we can get to where we want to go. We need to force ourselves in the direction we decide and not wander, like space rocks, toward whatever or whomever pulls us harder. In order to move toward a goal or destination, we need to find fuel to create a force to move us forward.

A Bloody Feel-Good Story: The Preparation and Mindset of a Champion

Jacob "Stitch" Duran is a Puerto Rican migrant farmworker who became "everyone's favorite cut man."[26] Working for the Ultimate Fighting Championship (UFC) and other MMA organizations, Stich is responsible for preventing and treating damage to fighters in full-contact sports. He has less than one minute between rounds to fix a deep gash, a broken nose, or even an open artery. Every second counts, and his expertise has saved more than a few bouts from being stopped due to an injury. He not only does it for a living, but he is also the best in the world at it.

Can you really look deeply into another person's soul? If it were truly possible, I suppose no one would have more practice than Stitch. In an interview, he told me:

> When I work a corner, and I see a fighter has nothing left, I look straight into his eyes, tell him to relax; now, this is where champions are made. It's 90 percent mental and 10 percent talent. If he has prepared properly, his body will respond. An MMA fighter entering the fight cage—the Octagon—is remarkably vulnerable, fully exposed to the watching world. In those moments, a close observer can discern a lot. These warriors have spent years working on every facet of martial arts, only to put it all on the line for a few moments in the cage. As

---

26 Katalin Rodriguez Ogren, "Stitch, MMA's Favorite Cutman, Gives Insight into a Dream Job," Pow! Martial Arts & Fitness, April 30, 2010, http://www. chicagonow.com/pow-martial-arts/2010/04/stitch-mmas-favorite-cutman-gives-insight-into-a-dream-job/.

they are exposed to the talents and violence of their opponents, their family, friends, coaches, and teammates look on. When I start wrapping a fighter's hands, reality sets in. It's showtime—he's going into battle.

A war begins in the next few minutes, and the person on the other side of the cage will try to destroy them physically and mentally, trying to take away their dreams. Before each fight and between the rounds, I often see fighters who may not be the most talented or the most skilled, but they have the heart to fight one more round—even when their bodies are crying out to give up. Same thing in life: you are not the only one on the ropes of life. Sometimes we have to challenge ourselves or go up against the system to get the things we want. You'll see negatives and positives in life. When there's a negative, you need to believe there'll be a positive right behind it.

CHAPTER 6
Stop the Loneliness Social Media Brings

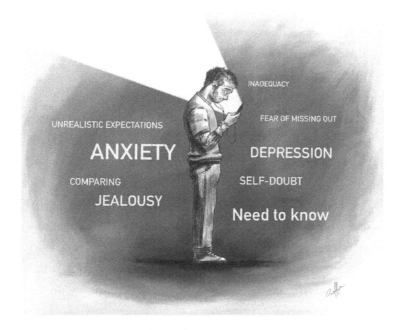

INADEQUACY

UNREALISTIC EXPECTATIONS

FEAR OF MISSING OUT

ANXIETY

DEPRESSION

COMPARING

SELF-DOUBT

JEALOUSY

Need to know

L et this be a wake-up call for all of us. The Centers for Disease Control and Prevention released their life expediency data for 2017. An article in *Investor's Business Daily* noted, "The life expediency of millennials is going down. The average American can expect to live to 78.6 years, the CDC said, down from 78.7 years in

2016."[27] This may not seem like much of a change, but we are heading in the wrong direction. The article goes on to state, "The last time such a drop happened in life expediency was from 1915 to 1918. That period coincided with World War I and the deadly Spanish flu epidemic, which together claimed 792,000 American lives."

So what has changed? Why would life expectancy decline in the age of modern medicine and at a time of relative peace? One element to consider is the hopelessness and low self-esteem that plagues millennials. Many turn to drugs for relief or see suicide as the only way to end the pain: "Suicide rates have soared by 33% from 1999 to 2017, data show. Suicide rates are at their highest in 50 years. Suicide is now the second-leading cause of death for ages 10 to 34, and the fourth leading cause for 35 to 54. And the opioid epidemic is taking a toll, as well. Deaths due to drug overdose have surged 10% in the last year alone, from 63,632 in 2016 to 70,237 in 2017. Since 1999, the drug overdose rate is up 255%."[28]

While addiction, mental illness, and suicide are complex issues, we can likely all agree that social media—and the anxiety and depression from the comparison and sense of "less than" that comes with it—is potentiallty a contributing factor. An extensive study out of London should alarm us all: "A massive 8 out of 10 millennials say they aren't 'good enough' in virtually all areas of their life, from health and love to their careers and relationships with peers. In fact, the pressure is so great that 79% of those polled said it was affecting their mental health."[29]

---

27 "Life Expectancy Decline: Have Young Americans Lost Hope Amid Plenty?," Investor's Business Daily, November 28, 2018, https://www.investors.com/politics/editorials/life-expectancy-decline-young-lost-generation/.

28 Ibid.

29 Jeff Parsons, "8 in 10 Millennials Believe They Aren't 'Good Enough' at Life," Metro, November 5, 2019, https://metro.co.uk/2019/11/05/8-10-millennials-believe-arent-good-enough-life-11044234/.

To me, social media addiction is the new chain smoking. As a little kid, I would go to work with my dad. We took the train and always went to the smoking car. As a ten-year-old watching men and women smoke on the way to the city, I'd think, *What idiots! Wasting their time and risking their health.* People today waste countless hours and perhaps jeopardize their health with the time spent staring into a screen.

According to *Social Media Today*, a leading industry publication that analyzes the latest happenings in the social media industry, the average person will check their phone one hundred and fifty times per day and spend nearly two hours (approximately 116 minutes) on social media every day.[30] My three children tell me the number is probably much higher, and many experts feel the total time spent each day will continue to increase as platforms develop. Ask yourself, is spending so much time on my phone getting me closer to my goals?

Overexposure to everything happening in the world, twenty-four hours a day, seven days a week, is a recipe for overwhelming stress. We're just not equipped to run as fast as the world seems to run at times, particularly when it comes to social media.

A study from the Intergenerational Foundation compared three generations of young people and found today's millennials are unhappier and lonelier than previous generations, reporting a lower sense of well-being across areas including health, relationships, and finances. According to the Bustle Company, "The investigation looked at five aspects of well-being—relationships, economics, health, personal environment, and belonging—in surveys conducted in 1995, 2005, and 2015, with all participants aged between 20 and 29. Sadly, the findings

---

30 Evan Asano, "How Much Time Do People Spend on Spcial Media? [Infographic]," SocialMediaToday, January 4, 2017, https://www. socialmediatoday.com/marketing/how-much-time-do-people-spend-social-media-infographic.

weren't positive. The study isn't the first to suggest a link between social media and poor mental health among young people."[31]

The clean eating trend, popularized on platforms like Instagram and YouTube, has been linked to the development of eating disorders. And *The Guardian* reports that a British study in 2017 found "Instagram, Facebook, Snapchat, and Twitter increased feelings of inadequacy and anxiety among 14- to 24-year-olds, with Instagram proving the most problematic."[32]

Overexposure to everything happening in the world,
twenty-four hours a day, seven days a week, is a recipe
for overwhelming stress.

Social media exacerbates FOMO, the fear of missing out, as we get trapped in social comparison, which can lead to depression and a heightened sense of loneliness.[33] Users become like zombies, missing out on healthy activities while watching the activity of others. Excessive internet use makes us lonely as we attempt to replace face-to-face relationships with online relationships. We temporarily feel better during online activity but soon find these connections tend to be superficial and

---

31 Emily Dixon, "Why Do I Feel So Lonely? Millennials Are Unhappier Than Previous Generations, According to New Research," Bustle, August, 10, 2018, https://www.bustle.com/p/why-do-i-feel-so-lonely-millennials-are-unhappier-than-previous-generations-according-to-new-research-10051122.

32 Denis Campbell, "Facebook and Twitter 'Harm Young People's Mental Health,' " The Guardian, May 19, 2017, https://www.theguardian.com/society/2017/may/19/popular-social-media-sites-harm-young-peoples-mental-health.

33 Gigen Mammoser, "The FOMO Is Read: How Social Media Increases Depression and Loneliness," Healthline, December 9, 2018, https://www.healthline.com/health-news/social-media-use-increases-depression-and-loneliness#Does-social-media-cause-depression.

ultimately unsatisfying. In addition, lonely people give more attention to negative social information, like disagreement or criticism. They recall more of the negative things that occurred during an encounter than positive things. All this leads, as you might imagine, to negative expectations about future interactions with others.[34]

Control social media, or, no doubt, it will control you.

As an old-school guy, I see social media as both good and bad, useful and harmful. It's great to have access to technology to make connections all over the world. However, you either control it, or, no doubt, it will control you. It can suck you into a make-believe world where you begin to question your own existence and why you are not living the perfect life. If you let it, social media can "download" a host of negative and harmful emotions into your mind.

At a minimum, social media is anything but social. Just sitting at dinner with my three children and my wife, I've noticed we are all looking down at our phones to see the latest snap or post from people we barely know.

Follow the Money

Dog bites man, not an eye-catching story. Man bites dog, now that's something that will get your attention. A certain segment of the population will say just about anything to get your attention to eventually get your money.

---

34   Ibid.

If you want to understand why something is happening,
follow the money.

According to a study done by Villanova University, "The global digital advertising space was worth $154 billion in 2015. By 2020, the industry will be worth over $250 billion."[35] In many areas of our society and economy, I have observed that if you want to understand why something is happening, you must follow the money.

The seemingly innocent smartphone you're looking at is not so innocent. In today's gig economy, marketers don't see you as a person but as a lead and potential consumer. Their job is to get to know you better than you know yourself, and, in many cases, they do. On one hand, even businesses like Facebook and Instagram deserve to get a return on their investment. It costs a fortune to create a social media platform that attracts billions of people around the world; it is no small task. It takes time, money, and resources, with no guarantee of profit. However, if you think these sites are "free," you are wrong. The price you pay for enjoying the platform is personal information as they track your every move, including location, demographics, age, gender, interests, behavior, and connections.

Catchy, witty headlines entice you to click on ads known as lead magnets. As you tap and surf, watch a video, or use an app, tracking technology is put to work. Your personal data information is being packaged and sold. They turn you and billions of people around the world into "big data." They understand your purchase history and

---

35   Richard Fry, Ruth Igielnik, and Eileen Patten, "How Millennials Today Compare with Their Grandparents 50 Years Ago," Pew Research Center, March 16, 2018, https://taxandbusinessonline.villanova.edu/blog/how-marketers-use-data-analytics-to-reach-customers/.

websites you have visited. In turn, this information is sold to other marketing companies.

Even Elon Musk

Elon Musk, CEO of Tesla and SpaceX, was interviewed by Joe Rogan on *The Joe Rogan Experience*. He said he had disconnected his Facebook and Instagram accounts while keeping Twitter as a way to communicate. Musk notes, "On social media, people look like they're having a better life than they really do. They modify pictures to look perfect. Then others say, why am I not that happy? I must suck!" Joe chimed in with a quote from Theodore Roosevelt, twenty-sixth president of the United States. What Teddy said way back then still holds true: "Comparison is the thief of joy."

"Comparison is the thief of joy."

And for the future, Elon shared a strong warning on Joe's podcast: "Artificial intelligence is already part of social media and will grow. The percentage of high level intelligence until now were humans. In the future intelligence particularly artificial intelligence will be far greater than humans. One thing is for sure, we will not control artificial intelligence." Joe Rogan's conclusion? He said, "We, as humans, will be looking at artificial intelligence as if it is a god, and we will beg, 'We just want to go back!' "

Elon has warned President Obama and Congress about the dangers of artificial intelligence. His advice was pretty much ignored. So, now Elon says, "If you can't beat them, then join them."[36] Though he thinks artificial intelligence is dangerous, he started a company called Neuralink, proving Musk is willing to go along for a profit. Neuralink's goal is to blend technology and the human brain.

Joe Rogan, in his interview with Musk, questioned where technology may be taking us as a society:

The future is a combination of biology (living things) and electronics (technology). We are already using AI in phones; now imagine what you can do with your phone you could do with your brain just by thinking . . . We may be living in virtual reality in the future, where you can't tell what's real and what's not real. Maybe our desire to keep moving forward with technology will one day be the downfall of mankind. If an outsider would look at humans, they would easily conclude we are a flawed system . . . lies, cheats, wars, and more. To an artificial intelligence, we may be so flawed it would want to get rid of us.

Control the False World

Even a former Facebook executive, Chamath Palihapitiya, has said he feels "tremendous guilt" over his work on "tools that are ripping apart the social fabric of how society works," joining a growing chorus of critics of the social media giant. Palihapitiya, who was vice president for user growth at Facebook, said, "The short-term, dopamine-driven feedback loops that we have created are destroying how society works. Your behaviors, you don't realize it, but you are being programmed. It

---

36 Daniela Hernandez and Heather Mack, "Elon Musk's Neuralink Shows Off Advances to Brain-Computer Interface," *The Wall Street Journal*, July 17, 2019, https://www.wsj.com/articles/elon-musks-neuralink-advances-brain-computer-interface-11563334987.

was unintentional, but now you gotta decide how much you're going to give up, how much of your intellectual independence."[37]

"The short-term, dopamine-driven feedback loops that we have created are destroying how society works."
—Chamath Palihapitiya, Facebook

And for you Instagram lovers, be aware that in March 2012 Facebook bought Instagram for $1 billion. A study by Harvard University in 2018 shows an increase in dopamine activity in the brain while on social media: "Dopamine is a chemical produced by our brains that plays a starring role in motivating behavior. It gets released when we take a bite of delicious food, when we have sex, after we exercise, and, importantly, when we have successful social interactions. In an evolutionary context, it rewards us for beneficial behaviors and motivates us to repeat them."[38] In other words, tapping on our phones can be highly addictive and like any addiction there could be a personal price to pay.

Keep in mind, your mental health is the engine that will help you navigate through life. If social media makes you feel inadequate, shut it down. You'll find freedom in not caring what others do, say, or think. Don't fall into the trap of one-upping your peers or turning every moment into an opportunity to prove your worthiness to the world. Having grown up with social media, your generation faces this temptation daily, hourly.

---

37 Julia Carrie Wong, "Former Facebook Executive: Social Media Is Ripping Society Apart," *The Guardian*, December 12, 2017, https://www.theguardian.com/technology/2017/dec/11/facebook-former-executive-ripping-society-apart.

38 Trevor Haynes, "Dopamine, Smartphones, & You: A Battle for Your Time," Harvard Unversity, May 1, 2018, http://sitn.hms.harvard.edu/flash/2018/dopamine-smartphones-battle-time/.

The advice I have for you is this: let go of who you think you're supposed to be (according to others) and embrace who you are. Don't judge your self-worth on likes, shares, comments, snaps, or emojis. Think about it. Do you really want a screen to have a negative impact on your life? You'll face enough real problems in life, with family, work, relationships, finances, and health. Let's stop manufacturing drama online. Let's stop stressing over how our virtual personas are perceived.

In the past, you have learned to set limits on other things in your life. Limits on drinking, eating, or shopping are necessary for a healthy life. Same thing for social media. Set limits, have priorities. Turn off "push" notifications. If you want to see the latest, log in. Don't set yourself up to get notifications 24/7. Let technology work for you when you say and how you say.

UFC commentator, comedian, and podcast host Joe Rogan's strategy is "post and drop," meaning you post, walk away, and don't read the comments. Joe offered this encouragement on his podcast, *The Joe Rogan Experience*: "If you feel like you have something positive to offer, don't worry about the minority, who really are just a bunch of a-holes. Chances are, they are doing it to you and many others . . . ignore them."

Social media can be a false world with people trying to prove their significance. Comparing your life to others' will create thoughts of jealously. If you feel social media is affecting your feelings about yourself, than look at it like an enemy and treat it like an enemy. Back off, and begin the process of distancing yourself from it.

Review the comments you post on social media. Are you proud of them? Have you shown empathy and compassion? Have you followed the "golden rule" of treating others the way you want to be treated? Or have you been sucked into negativity and written things you shouldn't have? Remember, all you post, even if deleted, can be found later. Whatever you write, assume your family, business colleagues, and friends will see it—even future employers, college admission offices, or your future mate. Using such a public forum for negative or inappropriate content is sure to be a future regret.

Read a book, listen to music, exercise, meditate, or fly a kite—
anything that will give your brain a break.

I feel bad for your generation. Youth is often the time for stupid, immature mistakes. Now, cameras are everywhere, capturing and preserving your missteps. Sure, camera phones have benefits; however, they can have a severe downside. You make a mistake—perhaps a one-time event or even the worst moment of your life—and it can be posted on a social media platform for the public to see. Add to that risk the emotional cost of always being connected, of never having a break from your peers. When I was a kid, I was often bullied at school, but when I went home, I was safe. This isn't always true now, with the relatively new phenomena of cyberbulling.

And smartphones distort our work/life balance. I worked hard starting out, but most of my early jobs were the traditional hours of nine o'clock to five. Now it's almost expected that employees will be online to take care of business at a moment's notice. Even a vacation is not what it used to be. When I was your age, if you went to the beach or mountains to get away, you really were away. Now, vacations are all about posting on Snapchat, Instagram, and Facebook. The rush to let others know our every move means we lose out on much-needed personal downtime.

Check in less and break the unproductive cycle of social media addiction. Disconnect from your phone and reconnect with family and friends. Check a maximum of three times per day. Set a timer. Go to your settings and limit yourself to under an hour a day on social media. You will get reminders as you approach your limit.

Put yourself in the future. Do you want to look back in five years and feel a sense of loss as you realize how much time you wasted on the superficial? The time to put limits in place is now.

According to the Pew Research Center, 22 percent of all Americans use Twitter. It's also estimated that 10 percent of the users make up 80 percent of the tweets.[39] Therefore, you are really only hearing from a very small minority, whether on Facebook, Instagram, or some new platform that comes up. The loud and obnoxious users are heard more often. Your hobby should not be viewing social media posts. If it is, get a new hobby. Step away from the ignorance. Read a book, listen to music, exercise, meditate, or fly a kite—anything that will give you a brain break.

Social Media Apps Traced Back More Than Three Thousand Years

In 2019 my family and I visited Egypt. We spent about ten days traveling to ancient sites, from Giza's colossal pyramids to the Great Sphinx to Luxor's hieroglyph-lined Karnak Temple to the Valley of the Kings and the Temple of Horus. We also spent time in the capital city of Cairo and visited several mosques. We had the pleasure of sailing down the Nile River from the town of Aswan. Ramses II's great temple of Abu Simbel was particularly spectacular. It featured a colossal statuary standing guard outside and an interior wonderfully decorated with wall paintings dating back to about 1264-1244 BCE.[40]

The final leg of the trip was a visit to the Egyptian Museum in Cairo. The golden glory of King Tutankhamun and the fascinating exhibits of royal mummies are all part of this impressive museum's tour.

---

39   Adam Hughes and Stefan Wojcik, "Key Takeaways from Our New Study of How Americans Use Twitter," Pew Research Center, April 24, 2019, https://www.pewresearch.org/fact-tank/2019/04/24/key-takeaways-from-our-new-study-of-how-americans-use-twitter/.
40   Joshua J. Mark, "Abu Simbel," Ancient History Encyclopedia, May 9, 2018, https://www.ancient.eu/Abu_Simbel/.

In processing all we saw, I came to realize that none of the kings, pharaohs, or warriors depicted in art, statues, or hieroglyphics were overweight or bore imperfections. They were all young, strong, and fit. Our tour guide was Ismail Ahmed Gamea, an Egyptologist and professor. Egyptology is the study of ancient Egyptian history, language, literature, religion, architecture, and art from the fifth millennium BC until fourth century AD.[41]

I simply asked our guide, "Why is it that these kings are all so fit and handsome?" He said, "They instructed the stonecutters to carve their image the way they wanted to be perceived by society. Pharaohs were seen as gods or semigods, so they were depicted as perfect figures." Thus, most of ancient Egyptian art is known as idealistic art (except the Akhenaton Era, 1353-1336 BCE, in which art was more realistic).[42]

This approach to art reminds me of the many Photoshop-like apps we use on our smartphones, like Facetune. This simple app lets the user use filters to make his image look as close to "'perfect'" as possible. You can add more detail to the face or change its shape (yes, really), patch up imperfections on the skin, whiten teeth, and much more.[43]

I was also curious why humans and animals were combined in Egyptian art. Ismail explained, "Pharaohs usually had human form, but sometimes they were represented by a combination of human and animal form, like the Sphinx, which represents the king as a combination of power and intelligence. Its form says the king should be as strong as a lion and as smart as a human. In artwork, vultures and cobras were also symbols of protection and power." To me, this sounds like the app

---

41 "Egyptology," *Wikipedia* page, last updated August 18, 2019, https://en.wikipedia.org/wiki/Egyptology.

42 Joshua J. Mark, "Akhenaten," Ancient History Encyclopedia, April 17, 2014, https://www.ancient.eu/Akhenaten/.

43 Hillel Fuld, "Facetune Is an iOS Photo-Editing App That Can Truly Be Called Magical," HuffPost, December 6, 2017, https://www.huffpost.com/entry/facetune-is-an-ios-photoe_b_3501920.

Snapchat, which uses filters so the user can have a tongue like a dog, hair like a rock star, or a flower crown on her head.[44]

Doing more research, it seems that Egyptian pharaohs were often overweight and not as healthy as portrayed: "Egyptian art commonly depicts pharaohs as being trim and statuesque, but this was most likely not the case. The Egyptian diet of beer, wine, bread, and honey was high in sugar, and studies show that it may have done a number on royal waistlines. Examinations of mummies have indicated that many Egyptian rulers were unhealthy and overweight, and even suffered from diabetes."[45]

Even King Tutt was a bit different than the splendid, strapping king portrayed by his tomb. A new DNA study found King Tut was a frail pharaoh, beset by malaria and a bone disorder. Carsten Pusch, a geneticist at Germany's University of Tübingen, describes him this way: "He was not riding the chariots . . . Picture instead a frail, weak boy who had a bit of a club foot and who needed a cane to walk."[46]

R. Kay Green posted a blog on Huffington Post stating, "As we know, perception is everything; especially in the world of social media. In terms of perception, we all have an ideal self. We all wish to maximize our careers, our profession, and aspire to be like those who we find most successful. As the use of social media continues to evolve, the concept of presenting our ideal selves versus our real selves has become more and more prevalent on social media platforms such as Facebook, Twitter, Instagram, Pinterest, and even LinkedIn. From a societal standpoint,

---

44   Dani Marsland, "The Secrets behind How Your Fave Snapchat Filters Work: It's Doggone Amazing," Pile Rats, http://pilerats.com/written/light-easy/the-secrets-behind-how-your-fave-snapchat-filters-work/.

45   Evan Andrews, "11 Things You May Not Know About Ancient Egypt," History. com, August 29, 2012, https://www.history.com/news/11-things-you-may-not-know-about-ancient-egypt.

46   Ker Than, "King Tut Mysteries Solved: Was Disabled, Malarial, and Inbred," National Geographic, February, 17, 2010, https://www.nationalgeographic.com/news/2010/2/100216-king-tut-malaria-bones-inbred-tutankhamun/.

many of us are driven by competition, achievement, and status; hence, the creation and portrayal of our hyperidealistic selves."[47] For many social media users, it is an esteem booster, which explains why so many people spend so much time on social media. It provides many individuals with a false sense of self and an inflated sense of who they really are.

My point is, insecurity is not a new personality trait. It probably dates back to the beginning of mankind. Humans are hardwired to feel a variety of emotions. When you're on social media and feel a decrease in self-esteem and an increase in self-doubt and inadequacy, it's time to log off and do something that truly makes you happy.

---

47   R.Kay Green, "The Social Media Effect: Are You Really Who You Portray Online?" HuffPost, October 7, 2013, https://www.huffpost.com/entry/the-social-media-effect-a_b_3721029.

CHAPTER 7
People Skills in a Technology- Driven Society

D aily, we are surrounded by information to process and choices to make. Our news feeds tell us to eat this, buy that, and become them. We are bombarded with messaging to the point that our mental hard drive becomes overwhelmed. The content we swipe through breezes by so quickly we barely have time to absorb any true meaning. We have evolved into an immediate, now society, always searching for instant gratification. When it doesn't happen, we are disappointed. We've forgotten how to live life in real time. We want a faster, easier version of living and satisfaction. One of the consequences of this shift is that many of us are losing the art of people skills.

Our smartphone society, and the lack of interpersonal know-how it brings, leads many people down a path of social awkwardness . . . But few things are better than having a one-on-one conversation that ends with a hug. A smartphone can't provide that.

When I was growing up, if you didn't have people skills, you would struggle in life. I think I had it easier than most. The majority of my early jobs were either sales or as a bouncer and bartender. If I didn't learn how to relate to people early on, my nights at the bar would have resulted in many more fights. At eighteen, I had my first sales job, selling vacuums door-to-door; I would've been a complete failure without the ability to communicate one-on-one—which can only be learned through practice, talking to people face-to-face. Trust me when I tell you, you need people skills to knock on a complete stranger's door and sell them a $500 vacuum.

Now, as a business owner, I've had hundreds of people work for me over the years. Social skills are a must. At times, I've felt more like a sociologist than anything else. Interpersonal communication has proven paramount to the success I've had.

Our smartphone society, with its lack of interpersonal know-how, leads many people down a path of social awkwardness and social anxiety and produces a heavy, empty feeling in their day-to-day interactions. The trend toward fewer intimate, emotionally connected relationships will no doubt continue. With an abundance of artificial connection through artificial intelligence—robots, holograms, virtual reality, and the introduction of 5G—we may gradually feel less compelled to prioritize person-to-person communication.

I strongly disagree with this trend. Few things are better than having a one-on-one conversation that ends with a hug. A smartphone can't provide that.

Listen Your Way to a Better You

Phones pull us into the virtual world and out of the world around us. Have you ever had someone who wanted to talk to you—a spouse, coworker, or child—but you didn't look up from your device to truly hear what they had to say? Most likely, you didn't hear them well and they felt devalued. Have we forgotten how to listen, how to make the other feel heard?

I've learned one of the most important parts of communicating is the ability to listen well, without distraction. We all share the need to be heard, to feel our words and thoughts matter to another. Listening is one of the most sincere forms of respect. Sometimes listening is the only thing needed to help someone. People are guided by their emotions and have an innate drive to share them. Listening is about being present and putting your agenda on the sidelines.

In general, good people skills are defined as the ability to listen, to communicate, and to relate to others on a personal or professional level. What else will listening do? It will give you the ability to show empathy; this is the capacity to understand or feel what another person is experiencing from within their frame of reference. If you can show that you truly care about somebody else's feelings and they believe you do, they feel important. When you won't look up from your screen to look into the eyes of another, it sends a message of disregard. Is that what you are trying to communicate?

Feel-Good Story: Howard Stern

All too often, we start a conversation, briefly hear the issue of the person across from us, and, before you know it, we throw our "tale of woe" into the conversation, completely hijacking and derailing what may be important to the person you are speaking with.

I sat across from "King of All Media" Howard Stern during an advertising meeting—just me, him, and a sales rep. Howard said one thing as we began, but then he just listened. He said, "How can I help you sell more of the art you're trying to sell?" I went on for ten minutes about all he could say on his radio show. Howard listed intently without interrupting. He said, "I got all I need," and within a week, our ads ran on Howard's show. Needless to say, it was a grand slam.

Because Howard listened, he was able to convey the message we wanted to convey. We advertised on his show for years, bringing in big bucks. I was invited to a couple of his birthday parties, and it was all possible because two individuals sat across from each other and created a win-win situation.

Another great lesson from Howard about communication was in his follow-up. Howard didn't need to send me a handwritten letter—particularly being in his position—but he did. It read, "Thanks for your support of the show; let's eliminate the competition." Do you think that inspired me to spend more money with Howard? Yes, it did, and the note still hangs on my wall.

Don't Be Daffy Duck

I grew up watching Warner Brothers' cartoon character Daffy Duck. He was all about me-me-me and mine-mine-mine. That attitude and those communication "skills" didn't work for Daffy. (Bugs Bunny always got the upper hand.) Focusing on your wants and your preferences won't work for you either. Don't be a Daffy Duck.

Don't live in a bubble. Have conversations with people from all walks of life, not just your immediate circle. Be willing to learn from others. Chances are, if you show you care what they have to say, they will do the same for you.

No more prejudging people. Give everybody an opportunity. Judge others by their actions, not by your first impressions. Instead of points of disagreement, look for collaboration; strive to work together toward the common good. Set up deals where both parties come out a winner. These deals work out well over the long haul.

Make people feel like they're heard. You don't have to agree with their point of view to say, "I understand how you feel." Just letting somebody vent will go a long way.

If there's a conflict, don't try and resolve it by text. Texts have no context and are often misinterpreted by others. A text can't communicate tone or body language. Pick up the phone or, better yet, sit down with those with whom you need to resolve issues.

When speaking with someone, be in the present moment. Attuning to others and allowing them to talk without interruption may take practice and discipline. Interpersonal communication takes time and effort, but, like any other worthwhile pursuit, the hard work eventually pays off.

In business, build rapport. In addition to bringing a smile, consider bringing a small, thoughtful gift to a meeting (if company policy allows). Ask questions and listen to better understand the others' needs. A big part of getting what you want is helping other people get what they need.

Relationships are a mirror. If you are unhappy, chances are, the person in front of you is unhappy as well. Fix what's wrong for the benefit of both.

Take a pause before you speak, if only for a moment, to consider the consequences of your words. You may think better of what you were about to say if you give yourself time to reflect. And if you must speak strongly, it's a good idea to provide your point of view with a little sweetness.

CHAPTER 8
The Ultimate Gift to Yourself

What the $90 Billion Man Says About Health

Legendary investor Warren Buffet once said of his health, "If I were to give you any car you wanted, no matter the price, for free, would you take it? The answer is obviously yes. The only catch is you would have to keep that car for your entire life. Just as you would take care of that car is the mindset how you should take care of your health and body."

As far as I am concerned, the best investment you can make in life is the investment in your health. As a graduate with a degree in food science and a lifelong fitness fanatic, I was amazed when I read the report put together by Health System tracker that the United States spends almost double what any other developed country spends on health care,[48] yet according to The Bloomberg Global Health Index the US is only ranked 35th in overall health.[49]

Given our culture and society, when it comes to good health practices, the odds are stacked against us. The average age of death in the United States is now lower due to the opioid epidemic and suicide.

---

48 "How Does Health Spending in the U.S. Compare to Other Countries?" Peterson-Kaiser Health System Tracker, https://www.healthsystemtracker.org/chart-collection/health-spending-u-s-compare-countries/#item-start.
49 "Healthiest Countries 2019, World Population Review, 2019, http://worldpopulationreview.com/countries/healthiest-countries/.

Gun violence, climate change, and mental health concerns have led to a new description for millennials: "generation stress."[50] Stress affects how we feel and how effective we are by provoking a cascade of hormonal activity that can wreak havoc on your system.

Studies suggest chronic stress weakens the immune system, leaving you more susceptible to colds, viruses, and influenza.[51] Stress can flare up asthma, intensify skin conditions—such as eczema—and contribute to mental health issues, like anxiety and depression. It's a major cause of insomnia, which can lead to a host of other health problems.

So let's all agree that the responsibility for your health and well-being falls directly in your lap. It's perhaps the biggest lifelong commitment you take on. According to the American Psychological Association, millennials experience more stress and are less able to manage it than any other generation before them: "Their overexposure to everything happening in the world, twenty-four hours a day, seven days a week–literally their whole lives–is contributing to millennials' inability to turn things off, including their thoughts."[52]

I remember my ten-year high school reunion. I was shocked to see how my classmates had aged. I couldn't do too much to maintain my hairline, but I learned how to control my waistline. This healthy lifestyle has served me well. Now approaching sixty, I am still very competitive. I hit the weights, run sprints, and continue my love of martial arts. Don't ever think it's too late.

---

50   Don Joseph Goewey, "Generation Stress (Millennials and Gen X)," HuffPost, April 23, 2017, https://www.huffpost.com/entry/generation-stress-millennials-and-gen-x_b_58fcd956e4b0f02c3870eb99.

51   Razali Salleh Mohd, "Life Event, Stress and Illness," *Malaysian Journal of Medical Science*, Vol. 15, no. 4, (October, 2008), https://www.ncbi.nlm.nih.gov/pmc/articles/PMC3341916/.

52   "Stress by Generation," American Psychological Association, https://www.apa.org/news/press/releases/stress/2012/generations.

If you're looking for a magic pill to slow aging, I have it for you in a single word: *consistency*.

My father in-law, Dr. Jerry Levine, always said, "Don't put an old man in your body." I could not agree with him more. Keep young both physically and mentally. Like so many other things you will deal with in the course of your life, this "battle" will be you against yourself. Often you will not want to eat well; you will easily blow off the gym; you will justify bad habits and come up with convenient excuses. If this negligence is not kept in check, it will eventually result in a body and mindset that will not serve you well.

As a young person you can "get away" with not eating as you should. However, your metabolism will slow down as time goes on. According to Kristen F. Gradney, RD, director of nutrition and metabolic services at Our Lady of the Lake Regional Medical Center and spokesperson for the Academy of Nutrition and Dietetics, "It is an actual fact that metabolism changes over time. It happens more progressively over time." That's because it's preempted by hormonal shifts that happen slowly as we go through life—it's not overnight.[53] So what does this mean for you? Start a healthy lifestyle when you're young and strong. Delay the aging process!

If you're looking for a magic pill to slow aging, I have it for you in a single word: *consistency*. Consistency will help you develop routines and build momentum toward anything in life you desire.

---

53   Amy Marturana, "The Truth About How Your Metabolism Changes as You Age," *Self*, November 10, 2016, https://www.self.com/story/how-metabolism-changes-as-you-age.

The Five Titans of Health

#1: Stay Physically Fit

It might surprise you to find out that early humans traveled as much as twelve miles a day while people today walk an average of less than half a mile.[54] I can't overemphasize the importance of physical activity and the effect it has on your success. Physical fitness should be a priority. The correlation between a strong mindset and physical fitness has been proven in numerous studies. The benefits reach far beyond improving your alertness and overall health; your sense of self-worth, pride, optimism, energy, and happiness are heightened within your soul. It improves creativity, fights depression, and trains you to take on demanding challenges.

For most healthy adults, the Department of Health and Human Services recommends these exercise guidelines: "Aerobic activity. Get at least one hundred and fifty minutes of moderate aerobic activity or seventy-five minutes of vigorous aerobic activity a week or a combination of moderate and vigorous activity."[55] This comes out to an average of twenty minutes a day of moderate aerobic activity or ten minutes per day vigorous aerobic activity. Ten minutes may not seem like a lot, but try doing sprints for ten minutes; you will feel the benefits.

Here's why. "Sprinting increases your metabolism more than jogging does and you can expect to burn more fat in the hours after the run. This is because after exercise, your body goes through a process called EPOC (excess post-exercise oxygen consumption). During this process your body uses fat as its primary source of energy and the more intense your workout, the more fat that gets burned in the hours after the run. This is

---

54   Stacy Hackner, "How Many Miles Did Early Humans Walk in a Day?," Quora, https://www.quora.com/How-many-miles-did-early-humans-walk-in-a-day.

55   "Physical Activity Guidelines for Americans," HHS.gov, https://www.hhs.gov/fitness/be-active/physical-activity-guidelines-for-americans/index.html.

why even though jogging at about 30-50% your VO2 max actually burns more fat than a sprint during the actual run, when you include the hours AFTER the run sprinting will burn more fat and calories overall."[56]

The *American Journal of Physiology* backs this claim up. In a study, a high-exercise group was instructed to exercise hard enough to produce a sweat, like from running or cycling, for sixty minutes a day. The moderate group only had to sweat for thirty minutes a day. The extra thirty minutes of exercise did not appear to provide any additional weight loss in body weight or fat.[57] For those who don't like traditional exercise, try gardening, dancing, active video games, or walking. The options go on and on. Get an accountability buddy to help you make strides toward your goals.

Through exercise, you will learn your body and mind are capable of more than you ever imagined.

Find your baseline. If you're looking to get in better shape, the first thing exercise experts recommend is to determine your fitness baseline, which is your current physical fitness level. This will give you a point of reference to measure your progress as you work toward your fitness goals. Measure weight, blood pressure, body fat percentage, and resting heart rate to have a beginning baseline. Every few months, measure your progress, and you will see that the more effort you put in, the better your overall fitness will become.

---

56 "Sprinting vs Jogging: Which Gets You a Better Body?," MaxMyLooks, https://maxmylooks.com/sprinting-vs-jogging/.

57 Jennifer Warner, "30 Minutes of Daily Exercise Enough to Shed Pounds," August 24, 2012, https://www.webmd.com/fitness-exercise/news/20120824/30-minutes-daily-exercise-shed-pounds.

If you haven't made exercise a part of your everyday activity, don't worry about it, but now is the time. The payoff is too big to ignore this area of your life any longer. Stop using excuses or putting up artificial barriers that prevent you from doing what you can. If you're concerned about failure, don't be. While you can learn certain things from success, the more valuable lessons are learned from failure. Through exercise, you will learn your body and mind are capable of more than you ever imagined.

#2: No Sleep, No Peace

In 1735 Benjamin Franklin said, "Early to bed, early to rise makes a man healthy, wealthy, and wise." More than 285 years later, this thought still holds true.

While you rest, your brain stays busy, overseeing biological maintenance that keeps your body running in top condition, preparing you for the day ahead.

According to HelpGuide.org, "While sleep requirements vary slightly from person to person, most healthy adults need between 7 to 9 hours of sleep per night to function at their best." Why is sleep so important? "The quality of your sleep directly affects your mental and physical health and the quality of your waking life, including your productivity, emotional balance, brain and heart health, immune system, creativity, vitality, and even your weight. Without enough hours of restorative sleep, you won't be able to work, learn, create, and communicate at a level even close to your true potential."[58]

---

58   "Sleep Needs," HelpGuide, https://www.helpguide.org/articles/sleep/sleep-needs-get-the-sleep-you-need.htm.

According to a study done by Nature Communications, the benefits of sleep could be vast. The brain needs to be less active to fight off infection. During sleep our DNA is repaired from radiation and other toxic elements. The *Journal of American College of Cardiology* sees an increase in heart disease with those who get less than six hours of sleep per night. According to the US Department of Transportation, sleep drowsiness causes approximately 20 percent of fatal crashes. It's like driving drunk with blood alcohol one-and-a-half times higher than the legal limit.[59]

Let's face it. If you're anything like me, even missing a few hours of sleep can make you angry or depressed. No other activity delivers so many benefits with so little effort. Sleep isn't merely a time when your body shuts off. While you rest, your brain stays busy, overseeing biological maintenance that keeps your body running in top condition, preparing you for the day ahead.

My Personal Story: Desperate for Hope, Sleep, and Peace

To say I am proud of the business I've built would be an understatement. As a below-average student in high school and college, I figured out a way to start a small art publishing company. Over the course of twenty-five years, I employed hundreds of people, many of whom stayed with me for decades. We signed licensing agreements with some of the greatest celebrities, athletes, and movie studios in the world.

Then one day, *boom*. I was accused of deliberately buying or arranging forgeries that accompanied some of our artwork. The weight of the world came tumbling down on me. I was ambushed by the media, confronted in court (lawsuit), and accused of committing a crime by people I never met (not the authorities). Individuals who had connections in all the

---

59 "Drowsy Driving," NHTSA, https://www.nhtsa.gov/risky-driving/drowsy-driving.

right places got the FBI involved. (I never had any ill will against the Bureau; they had no choice, considering the accusations against me.) A full and thorough investigation of my business was performed. With the help of a great staff (cheers for Agnes Palmer), I always ran a clean business. We kept good records and receipts to back up all purchases and signings. Though cleared, my empathy for those who have been falsely accused rose dramatically.

The problem was, for over two years, I was under extreme stress. Trying to get a good night's sleep was nearly impossible. During the day, my wife, Brooke, helped me survive this horror, and we were able to shield our young children. So as far as they knew, life was peachy. But at night I would replay the worst of the day's events. I would curl up in a ball, trying to understand how I'd endure the next day.

I needed to come up with a sleep strategy. A good friend (Ben) who lost his brother in a motorcycle accident sent me a book called *The Greatest Salesman in the World* by Og Mandino. Don't let the title fool you; it has little to do with sales and much to do with drilling an optimistic mindset deep into your brain. Ben wrote in the book, "Jerry, this book helped me survive the toughest time in my life. Use it, and you too will survive."

The book helped me so much. As simple as it sounds, I downloaded the audio version and listed over and over through the night. The setting of the story takes place thousands of years ago, so the narrator has an old, raspy voice, which made it all seem that much more authentic. Listening to this recording gave me hope and distracted me from my negative thoughts. I remember saying to myself in the middle of the night, "I don't know when or how, but I know there is a finish line out there with my name on it, and I will not stop until I get there."

I'm not sure if this book or this strategy will help you, but give it a try. To get to sleep, I try to listen to things I've already heard, even something boring. I don't want to stimulate my mind with new ideas while trying to calm myself for sleep. I listen to a podcast or a movie I have seen a hundred times—something that will calm me and lull me to sleep.

To create the best conditions for restful slumber, you also need to consider your sound environment. You may want to bring "white noise" into the bedroom. White noise is random noise that has a flat spectral density. That is, white noise has the same amplitude, or intensity, throughout the audible frequency range.[60]

White noise can also help neutralize sporadic sounds that may wake you. In your bedroom, this soothing noise can be created by a sound conditioner, a fan, or an air purifier—by anything that provides a consistent, soothing backdrop throughout the night. White noise not only helps you fall asleep, but it can also help you stay asleep.

It's easy enough to google sleep strategies. You'll find a variety of approaches to try. Stick to a sleep schedule, meaning you keep the same bedtime and wake-up time each day, even on the weekends. This helps to regulate your body's clock and will eventually help you fall asleep and stay asleep for the night. Other tips include lowering the room temperature, practicing calm breathing, using relaxation yoga, or learning to meditate.

I certainly recommend setting up a sleep environment that works for you. My wife, Brooke, likes sleeping with the lights on. She likes the sun coming in, so she can be comfortable "like a cat on a windowsill." Me? I like it dark and quiet. Any light bothers me, so I have an eye mask right by my bed. As far as bedding, sheets, blanket, and pillows, if spending a few extra bucks makes you more comfortable, it's money worth spending. The moral of the story is, you need to find what works for you. We are not "one size fits all" when it comes to getting good

60   Joseph Castro, "What Is White Noise?," Live Science, July 29, 2013, https://www.livescience.com/38387-what-is-white-noise.html.

sleep. Test a few methods; learn what works for you. You will find a good, healthy sleep pays off big-time.

#3: Stress Relief

Let's face it, if you are constantly stressed out, the quality of your life will diminish. You could have the greatest job, friends, and family, but if you are carrying a load of stress on your back, it will eventually break your spirit. For me, I really don't know what I would do without exercise; it's my go-to stress relief. If I put in an hour at the gym, the immediate benefits are there, but the good feeling I get will last many more hours that follow.

Juan Carlos Santana, a friend and one of the world's leading authorities on training and performance, explains the "high" reported by recreational and professional athletes. He points out that exercise can release an assortment of amazing feel-good chemicals from your body's own internal pharmacy, thus reducing stress. These include endorphins, dopamine, BDNF (brain-derived neurotropic factor), and serotonin, all influencing your overall happiness, sleeping habits, and satisfaction. Aim to exercise consistently and notice an overall reduction in your perceived level of stress.

If you're fighting with loved ones or carrying guilt, resentment, anger, or any other negative emotions, get rid of them ASAP . . . stress reduction should be at the top of your list for a happy, healthy life.

If you're fighting with loved ones, carrying guilt, resentment, anger, or any other negative emotions, get rid of them ASAP. Being stressed for hours or days at a time needs to be off the table. When you have a problem, seek to find the solution. According to skillsyouneed.com, to reduce stress, you should reduce caffeine, alcohol, and nicotine. Indulge in physical activity, get more sleep, try relaxation techniques such as meditation, talk to someone, and keep a stress diary to manage your time. Stress reduction should be at the top of your list for a happy, healthy life.

Today's society is go, go, go; do, do, do; and be, be, be. And that's fine at times, but just like a balloon, if you fill it up with too much air (stress), it will burst; the same holds true for each one of us.

#4: Spirituality: Getting Inner Peace

My first book came up short. *The Common Thread of Overcoming Adversity and Living Your Dreams* was great for people who were motivated by the "No Pain, No Gain" attitude. Many hard-core, in-your-face individuals were featured. Their "do-it daily" tasks for the reader, including grit, bravery, fortitude, boldness, courage, and tenacity, were inspiring. But what if you are the type of person who just can't relate to those words or interject that tough mental mindset into your daily activities?

I asked myself, could there be a different pathway to achievement and success? The answer to that question came from my wife, Brooke. She enjoys and seeks to understand what the spiritual side, the universe, has to offer. I'm a bit more of a "realist," which sometimes limits my beliefs. Brooke appreciates the law of attraction and manifestation, and I wonder if these concepts or other spiritual aids could be helpful to you as well. Perhaps those who are not "hard core"—but still seek a sense of self-realization and completion—can tap into their spiritual side to reduce stress and increase happiness.

To Meditate or Not to Meditate

Perhaps you've heard others speak of meditation and have wondered how to start or if it might work for you. The Beatles brought attention to

Transcendental Meditation in the 1960s. TM was developed by Maharishi Mahesh Yogi and is now followed by many around the world, including Hugh Jackman, Lena Dunham, and Paul McCartney. Transcendental Meditation is described as a simple, natural, effortless meditation technique that doesn't involve contemplation or concentration.[61] One uses a mantra as a vehicle to let the mind settle down naturally and, ultimately, to transcend thought. According to the stats, between two hundred and five hundred million worldwide meditate.[62] Benefits include reducing stress, anxiety, depression, and pain. It also increases peace and well-being and may even help fight addictions. Research seeks to define meditation's possible health, psychological, neurological, and cardiovascular benefits.[63]

An Unlikely "Guru"

I was frustrated by my failed attempts at meditation, so I sought out advice. Dave Costen Jr. is a good friend, Brazilian jujitsu black belt, and yoga instructor. He put it to me simply: "You can't read about it; you need to experience it. And if it doesn't work the first time—like anything else—you must dedicate yourself to practicing it."

My journey started only a few miles from my house. Dave and I planned to meet and talk about self-awareness and spirituality. My first question to Dave was, "What does *enlighten* mean?" Dave said, "You mean like the book behind you?" I turned around, and on the shelf was

---

61   Deborah Varnetl, "The Difference between Transcendental Meditation & Mindfulness," LinkedIn, January 13, 2015, https://www.linkedin.com/pulse/difference-between-transcendental-meditation-deboragh-varnel-/.

62   "How Many People Meditate?," Mindworks, https://mindworks.org/blog/how-many-people-meditate.

63   Glenn N. Levine, et al, "Meditation and Cardiovascular Risk Reduction," *Journal of the American Heart Association*, Vol. 6, no. 10 (September 28, 2017), https://www.ahajournals.org/doi/10.1161/JAHA.117.002218.

a book called *Becoming Enlightened* by the Dalai Lama. Talk about the law of attraction!

We also happened to meet a very insightful man named Mark Atkinson, a Jamaican who embraces Rastafarian culture. Our conversation started when I asked him why he wears dreadlocks. He explained many Rastafarians believe that, like Samson, their hair is their strength, and it becomes a source of weakness if it is cut off.[64] As our conversation evolved, I became convinced Mark must be some type of spiritual guru. His answer to my question on meditation was impressive:

Why do I meditate? I will tell you . . . Mental and physical clarity. I am at peace. Meditation lets me escape from self-defeating thoughts. Nothing is going to be easy . . . It's been a fight for you before you were born. You started competing against millions of other sperms, and you won and were born! You survived illness, bullying, emotional trauma, and so much more! If you can do that, your attitude should be saying to yourself, *My best days are in front of me.* They will be if you let them. Meditation also lets me see that when I fail, I truly learn and become stronger. Your brain is a garden that will grow weeds. You need to get those weeds out and replace them with positive, productive thoughts . . . If you want to flourish, start today, start now.

Though Mark has found tremendous benefits through meditation, you may find other spiritual practices that speak to you. Whatever path you choose, it's hard to deny that man is body, mind, *and* spirit.

---

64 "Learn the Origins of the Dreadlocks Hairstyle," Jamaicans.com, https://jamaicans.com/dreadlocks/.

Therefore, we will fall short in our quest for improvement and health if we ignore this component.

Everything we *need* is supplied by nature . . . What we *want* has to be looked at carefully. We pay a price for the things we *want*. Ask yourself, is the price worth it?

Then I asked, "Okay, what about materialistic things? Isn't that a deep desire for most people?"

He replied, "It's fine, but what price are you paying? What stress is it bringing you? Is it worth it? You need to ask yourself, is the benefit worth it? Everything we *need* is supplied by nature . . . What we *want* has to be looked at carefully because we pay a price. Ask yourself, is the price worth it? I am not talking about hard work. It's good to work hard. I am talking about your ethics, your health, your family, your well-being."

All Meditation Is Not Created Equal

Then it came to me, "the secret door" was open. Listening to Mark, I realized there are many ways to meditate. Does it really matter how you get to your own spiritual place? As far as I am concerned, no. Mark benefited from meditation and described it as mental and physical clarity; escape from self-defeating thoughts; believing your best days are in front of you; and embracing failure as a chance to learn and become stronger.

I loved the image of my brain as a garden that will grow weeds. We all need to get those weeds out and replace them with positive, productive thoughts. Just like I have described self-esteem as an animal that needs to be feed, the same holds true for inner peace. It's an animal you need to feed and add to each day.

Define What Meditation Is for You

I believe if any of the traditional forms of meditation lets you escape from the daily grind, you must do it. You're always working out something in life. There is no finish line. So, having something you can rely on to add peace to your daily life is absolutely necessary. Finding what works for you is like a path through the forest. The first time you walk the path, you may not observe all it has to offer. If you're lucky, you will see some big trees, a tall mountain, and perhaps a stream. After you have walked on the same path many times, you will begin to see it's detail, variety, and beauty. The tiny wildflowers, the lush moss, and the abundance of little creatures. Each time you walk the path, you will see more and more of nature's wonders.

Having something you can rely on to add peace to your daily life is absolutely necessary.

In finding the "meditation" that works for you, the goal is to open your secret door to replace stress with inner peace. It is a singular thought or process that brings you from a dark place to a place of light where those little voices in your head can't get the best of you. When you discover it, treat it like the precious treasure it truly is.

What is it for you? What brings you peace? What provides sanctuary from the world?

- Yoga
- Praying
- Cooking
- Walking
- Music
- Journaling

- Hiking
- Gardening
- Baking

Find out what you really love to do and make sure you dedicate a portion of every day to your very own "great escape."

#5: Eat to Win

Google has plenty of great information concerning good eating habits. You don't need me for that: eat a variety of vegetables, fruits, whole grains, fat-free dairy products, lean meats, poultry, fish, beans, eggs, and nuts. Limit heavy-duty fats found in ice cream, cookies, and muffins. We've all heard this advice.

But I'd like to add a less popular piece of advice: do not go on a fad diet. I've been around a long time. Each year it seems another "miracle diet" markets itself as the "best ever." Don't believe the BS. These fad diets get you into the yo-yo syndrome of losing weight only to have it come storming back.

You should not be thinking "diet." It's about having a healthy lifestyle and maintaining a proper weight while providing your system with the necessary nutrients to give energy to your daily activities. The negative consequences of being overweight have been very well established: an increased chance of type 2 diabetes, high blood pressure, heart disease, and strokes, to name a few. And at the top of the heap for many is a negative view of themselves.

Perhaps hearing my journey will give you incentive to develop a long-term plan for health. As I write this book, I am pushing sixty, yet to me, it's just a number. I am just as strong as I have ever been, I believe, and am still a good athlete. In fact, I just finished my first Spartan Race. I roll (spar) at Brazilian jujitsu with guys half my age, and more times than not, I tap them out. I'm lucky because I found my why early on, and it has inspired me to keep pushing forward. Find your why and let it motivate you to eat well and stay in shape.

Find your why and let it motivate you to eat well
and stay in shape.

I knew I wanted to compete in sports and I knew that what I ate counted—and still counts today. The first book I ever read from cover to cover was *Eat to Win: The Sports Nutrition Bible* when it first came out in 1983. My mom and dad were fantastic parents, especially when it came to raising a bit of a nut like me. But their eating habits and overall outlook on health and wellness left something to be desired, so I had to figure this out on my own.

Each decade of my life, I've consistently stayed in shape with the foundation of eating well. This commitment has served me well, and I have no doubts that if you start early you will reap the benefits. The moral of the story is, I believe most of us know what we should and should not eat, but until you tap into your why and use it to keep you moving toward your goals, it's likely that, as you grow older, your health will deteriorate faster than it needs to.

Plan ahead so you can have the right foods around the house and designate go-to places on the road to stop for a quick, healthy bite. Put time and effort into understanding the ingredients in your food. Control your portion sizes. Drink water, not diet soda. Lay off the refined sugar; you don't need it in your body. Having a bad weekend or even a month—in the long run—is only a bump in the road. If you're consistent with your good eating habits over the years, the rest will take care of itself. Everything else is secondary.

Taking supplements and drinking red wine or green tea will not be a game changer for you. Avoid hyped-up products that claim you will have more energy or a better sex drive by taking what they're selling.

The good news is, millennials are much more aware of what they are eating than previous generations. They want to know what is in their food and how their food is made, demanding more information on food labels that will benefit all of us. The availability of foods that are natural, organic, and locally sourced is increasing each day—thanks, in no small part, to the millennial generation.

Substances and Your Health

As my own personal warning to you, watch out. I see many misleading health claims, all hoping to get into your pocketbook. Reminds me of how, years ago, tobacco was originally advertised with little concern for our health. The ads implied a message: smoke to be cool.

Marijuana

Cannabis claims many false benefits. (Remember, follow the money.) It's being marketed to today's youth in the form of gummy bears, cookies, and lollipops. Claims ranging from curing cancer to preventing Alzheimer's disease are touted. It's not that I don't believe medical benefit can be derived from some forms of marijuana. Cannabis can, to differing degrees, be used to treat a variety of medical issues, from back pain to seizures to the nausea associated with chemotherapy.

But risks are also associated with this drug, and the potential consequences have taken a back seat in most conversations. Marijuana has proven neurological and cardiovascular effects, impacts one's ability to drive, and hampers memory and learning. Heavy use can be harmful. Since pot smoke is chemically very similar to tobacco smoke, heavy pot smokers are at risk for some of the same health effects as cigarette smokers, like bronchitis and other respiratory illnesses.

My advice is, read the research. Trust empirical evidence, not a company who wants your money. No drug cures all. Take time to think through risks and benefits before you embrace the medical marijuana trend.

Vaping

Vaping, also known as *JUULing*, is becoming more popular with youth in middle school and high school. Vaping means using an electronic cigarette (e-cigarette) or other vaping device. E-cigarettes are battery powered and deliver nicotine through a liquid (called e-juice), which turns into a vapor when using the device. Researchers found that 92 percent of e-cigarettes studied contain diacetyl, a compound confirmed to cause popcorn lung.[65] Over time, it deteriorates lung function, and those with preexisting respiratory diseases (like asthma and COPD) who vape dramatically increase and expedite their risk of lung cancer (up to 15 percent higher than regular cigarettes, which we already know cause lung cancer). Formaldehyde, a confirmed carcinogen, is also another compound in e-cigarettes. Nicotine exposure from e-cigarettes may cause addiction and other adverse effects. Nicotine is regarded as a potentially lethal poison.

Concerns exist that vaping can cause harm by exposing users to toxic levels of nicotine. E-cigarette producers make enticing flavors to lure in teen users (piña colada, coffee, cherry, bubblegum, and more). Made with chemicals, but no tobacco, e-cigarettes are often marketed as a safe way to quit smoking. Yet, no difference in quitting rates were found among smokers who tried e-cigarettes versus those who didn't try them, according to a 2014 study in *JAMA/Medicine.*[66]

---

65   "Popcorn Lung: A Dangerous Risk of Flavored E-Cigarettes," American Lung Association, September 18, 2018, https://www.lung.org/about-us/blog/2016/07/popcorn-lung-risk-ecigs.html.

66   Rachel Grana, Neal Benowitz, Stanton A. Glantz, "E-Cigarettes: A Scientific Review," *Circulation*, Vol. 129, No. 2 (May 13, 2014) https://www.ncbi.nlm.nih.gov/pmc/articles/PMC4018182/.

And two recent studies, one in *The New England Journal of Medicine* and the other in *Nicotine & Tobacco Research*, found that many e-cigarettes still produce the carcinogenic compound formaldehyde, though in lower levels than regular cigarettes do.[67] There's also evidence that the chemicals used to create those alluring flavors could cause respiratory irritation in some cases.

Events have moved so quickly when it comes to the dangers of vaping. In 2018, when I first started researching the concerns of vaping, most of the thoughts were only theories. Toward mid-2019, the scary facts began to emerge. There have been over two thousand recorded cases of serious lung disease and at least thirty-nine deaths in twenty-four states.[68]

Recent CDC laboratory testing of bronchoalveolar lavage (BAL) fluid samples (or samples of fluid collected from the lungs) from twenty-nine patients with e-cigarette or vaping product use-associated lung injury (EVALI)[69] from ten states found vitamin E acetate in all of the BAL fluid samples. Vitamin E acetate is used as an additive in the production of e-cigarette or vaping products. This is the first time we have detected a potential chemical of concern in samples from patients with these lung injuries. The CDC continues to recommend that people should not use e-cigarette or vaping products that contain THC, particularly from informal sources like friends, family, or in-person or online dealers.

In layman's terms, vitamin E acetate seems fine for the skin or to digest, but when a person turns the vitamin E acetate into a vapor, it turns back to its original oil form once in the lungs. This process causes

---

67 Joseph G. Allen, "The Formaldehyde in Your E-Cigs," *The New York Times*, April 4, 2018, https://www.nytimes.com/2018/04/04/opinion/formaldehyde-diacetyl-e-cigs.html.

68 "Outbreak of Lung Injury Associated with the Use of E-Cigarette, or Vaping Products," Centers for Disease Control and Prevention, November 21, 2019, https://www.cdc.gov/tobacco/basic_information/e-cigarettes/severe-lung-disease.html.

69 "E-cigarette or Vaping Product Use-Associated Lung Injury (EVALI)," Yale Medicine, https://www.yalemedicine.org/conditions/evali/.

many victims to end up with acute respiratory distress syndrome, a life-threatening condition in which fluid builds up in the lungs and prevents oxygen from circulating in the bloodstream.[70]

Excessive Alcohol

Too much is being written about how red wine is good for you. In 1992, two Cornell University plant scientists suggested that resveratrol might be responsible for the cardiovascular benefits of red wine.[71] Throughout the book, I say to follow the money when something is being pushed on you. Companies standing to make a profit off red wine sales have taken the Cornell research, pumped it up, and tried to imply red wine can cure illness, etc.

Since then, hundreds of reports have indicated that resveratrol may—emphasis on *may*—protect against cancer, cardiovascular disease, vascular dementia, and Alzheimer's disease, thus extending the life span. This finding may hold true for moderate drinking, but it could also become a great excuse to overindulging.

According to alcohol.org, "Consuming too much alcohol can cause high blood pressure, irregular heartbeat, trouble pumping blood through the body, blood clots, stroke, cardiomyopathy (sagging heart muscle), heart attack, other heart disease, and breathing difficulty. Malnutrition from alcohol consumption can also lead to anemia."[72] So, you see, the stakes are high if you overindulge in alcohol regularly.

---

70   Hannah Knowles and Lena H. Sun, "What We Know About the Mysterious Vaping-Linked Illness and Deaths," *The Washington Post*, November 21, 2019, https://www.washingtonpost.com/health/2019/09/07/what-we-know-about-mysterious-vaping-linked-illnesses-deaths/.

71   Blaine Friedlander, "New York Red Wines Show Higher Levels of Resveratrol, a Cornell University Study Finds," Cornell Chronicle, February 2, 1998, https://news.cornell.edu/stories/1998/02/ny-red-wines-show-more-resveratrol.

72   "High Blood Pressure from Alcohol Consumption," alcohol.org, July 5, 2019, https://www.alcohol.org/effects/blood-pressure.

You want the benefits of resveratrol? No problem. It's found in foods such as peanuts, pistachios, red and white grapes, blueberries, cranberries, and even cocoa and dark chocolate. Those are, by far, safer sources of this organic compound.

Vitamins

In 2019, *Newsweek* reported a shocking take on the vitamin and supplement craze:

Popping vitamins and mineral supplements might feel virtuous, but it actually carries surprisingly few health benefits and could even do harm, according to researchers. A team of researchers in Canada found that common supplements such as multivitamins, vitamin D, calcium, and vitamin C provide no protection against heart disease, heart attack, stroke, or premature death.[73]

The study's lead author, Dr. David Jenkins of St. Michael's Hospital at the University of Toronto, said, "We were surprised to find so few positive effects for the most common supplements that people consume." While the review found that taking multivitamins, vitamin D, calcium, or vitamin C do no harm, "There is no apparent advantage either." Jenkins went on to conclude, "In the absence of significant positive data—apart from folic acid's potential reduction in the risk of stroke and heart disease—it's most beneficial to rely on a healthy diet to get your fill of vitamins and minerals. So far, no research on supplements has shown us anything better than healthy servings of less-processed plant foods, including vegetables, fruits, and nuts."[74]

---

73 "Most Popular Vitamin and Mineral Supplements Provide No Health Benefit, Study Finds," Science Daily, May 28, 2018, https://www.sciencedaily.com/releases/2018/05/180528171511.htm.
74 Ibid.

Opioids

The opioid epidemic is hitting millennials square in the face. According to the National Institute on Drug Abuse (NIDA), the opioid crisis is getting worse:

> Every day, more than 130 people in the United States die after overdosing on opioids. The misuse of and addiction to opioids—including prescription pain relievers, heroin, and synthetic opioids, such as fentanyl—is a serious national crisis that affects public health as well as social and economic welfare. The Centers for Disease Control and Prevention estimates that the total "economic burden" of prescription opioid misuse alone in the United States is $78.5 billion a year, including the costs of healthcare, lost productivity, addiction treatment, and criminal justice involvement.[75]

How did this happen? In February 2019, *60 Minutes* ran a feature on the crisis. Correspondent Bill Whitaker said, "In the late 1990s, pharmaceutical companies reassured the medical community that patients would not become addicted to prescription opioid pain relievers, and healthcare providers began to prescribe them at greater rates." Ed Thompson, a drug manufacturer who spent decades managing and producing opioids for big pharma, spoke with *60 Minutes* for this episode. His comments, which I've paraphrased below, are chilling:

> OxyContin was first approved in 1995. It was based on science that only showed it safe and effective when used "short term." But in 2001, pressured by Big Pharma and pain sufferers, the

---

75 "Opiod Overdose Crisis," NIH, January 2019, https://www.drugabuse.gov/drugs-abuse/opioids/opioid-overdose-crisis.

FDA made a fateful decision and, with no new science to back it up, expanded the use of OxyContin to just about anyone with chronic ailments like arthritis and back pain. The FDA did it by simply changing a few words on the label, that lengthy insert no one ever reads. Today the label says the powerful pain pills are effective for "daily, around-the-clock, long-term . . . treatment." And that small label change made a big change in the way drug companies would market all opioids, allowing them to sell more and more pills at higher and higher doses. This subsequently led to widespread diversion and misuse of these medications before it became clear that these medications could indeed be highly addictive. Opioid overdose rates began to increase. In 2017, more than 47,000 Americans died as a result of an opioid overdose, including prescription opioids, heroin, and illicitly manufactured fentanyl, a powerful synthetic opioid. That same year, an estimated 1.7 million people in the United States suffered from substance use disorders related to prescription opioid pain relievers, and 652,000 suffered from a heroin use disorder (not mutually exclusive).

These facts speak for themselves, so I probably don't have to tell you that opioids will wreck your life. All the potential you carry for success and a full, rich life is squandered if you lower your guard, thinking you can use but not abuse this deadly class of drugs.

Tobacco

As far as smoking is concerned—no way, no how! Read this quote from the American Lung Association as you consider the implications of tobacco use:

There are approximately 600 ingredients in cigarettes. When burned, they create more than 7,000 chemicals. At least 69 of these chemicals are known to cause cancer, and many are poisonous. Here are just a few: acetone (found in nail polish remover), arsenic (used in rat poison), benzene (found in rubber cement), butane (used in lighter fluid), and formaldehyde (used for embalming).[76]

Tobacco kills up to half of its users. Tobacco kills more than eight million people each year. More than seven million of those deaths are the result of direct tobacco use while around 1.2 million are the result of nonsmokers being exposed to secondhand smoke.[77]

As a sidenote, *prescribed medicines* are in a different category. Take them. According to the Centers for Disease Control and Prevention (CDC), a high cost is associated with not taking your medicines as prescribed: "The estimates [indicate] nonadherence causes 30 to 50 percent of chronic disease treatment failures and 125,000 deaths per year in this country. Twenty five to 50 percent of patients being treated with statins (cholesterol-lowering medications) who stop their therapy within one year have up to a 25 percent increased risk for dying."[78]

---

76 "What's in a Cigarette?" American Lung Association, https://www.lung.org/stop-smoking/smoking-facts/whats-in-a-cigarette.html.

77 "Tobacco," World Health Organization, July 26, 2019, https://www.who.int/news-room/fact-sheets/detail/tobacco.

78 Andrea B Neimah, et al, "CDC Grand Rounds; Improving Medication Adherence for Chronic Disease Management—Innovations and Opportunities," Centers for Disease Control and Prevention, November 17, 2017, https://www.cdc.gov/mmwr/volumes/66/wr/mm6645a2.htm.

CHAPTER 9
Building Your First Business

I used to explain my goal in business to my accountant, and he would always laugh. I would take my top hand and say, "The goal is to sell a product for as much as you can." Then I would take my lower hand and say, "And I try to keep my expenses as low as possible." I keep it simple.

So you can visualize and easily remember this fundamental truth in business, let's use the graphic below as a constant reminder of the importance of keeping profit high while concurrently keeping expenses low. Notice how the hands fit closely together; you need both parts of the equation to build a thriving business.

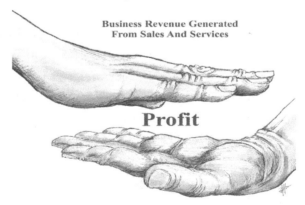

Business Revenue Generated From Sales And Services

Profit

Operating Expenses
Advertising   Fulfillment   Labor
Rent   Insurance   Cost of goods
The unforeseen

Making a profit is not always easy, but it is the key to creating a viable business. If your operating expenses (overhead) are too high and the revenue you generate from the business is too low, you will be out of business. Keep in mind, 50 percent of new businesses fail during the first five years.[79] Why? *Forbes* explains that "the inability to nail a profitable business model with proven revenue streams" is often the downfall of new ventures.[80]

Debt among nineteen- to twenty-nine-year-old Americans exceeded $1 trillion at the end of 2018, according to the New York Federal Reserve Consumer Credit Panel.[81] That's the highest debt exposure for the youngest adult group since late 2007. Student loans make up the majority of the $1,005,000,000,000 owed, followed by mortgage debt.

The goal in business (simplified): sell a product for as much as you can while keeping expenses as low as possible.

These numbers on debt among millennials make me passionate about encouraging and guiding you to start your own business. With a little coaching from me and persistence on your part, you can free yourself from the shackles of debt and realize your income goals. Once upon a time, starting your own business was difficult but not anymore. Like no other time in history, you have the power to employ yourself. Whether

---

79   Michael T. Deane, "Top 6 Reasons New Businesses Fail," Investopedia, June 25, 2019, https://www.investopedia.com/slide-show/top-6-reasons-new-businesses-fail/.

80   Eric T. Wagner, "Five Reasons 8 out of 10 Businesses Fail," Forbes, September 13, 2013, https://www.forbes.com/sites/ericwagner/2013/09/12/five-reasons-8-out-of-10-businesses-fail/#11adf28c6978.

81   "Total Household Debt Rises for 19th Straight Quarter, Now Nearly $1 Trillion Above Previous Peak," Federal Reserve Bank of New York, May 14, 2019, https://www.newyorkfed.org/newsevents/news/research/2019/20190514.

it be retail, wholesale, manufacturing, or building a service empire, the content I provide should prove useful and applicable for all business types. Let's start this chapter with an inspiring feel-good story. First we have to make you a believer; then, you will be ready to take action.

Note: As you read this chapter, if you are unsure about a word or phrase, please go to the end of this chapter and find the list of definitions I provide under "Financial Literacy."

A "Punkass" Feel-Good Story

TapouT founder Dan "Punkass" Caldwell didn't have any business experience or formula for creating a successful company. He grew up in San Bernardino, California, which he describes as the murder capital of the United States: "Drive-by shootings were regular occurrences. We had more murders per capita than any other place in the United States. My early life shaped me. I never felt in danger. I had good parents but not much money. I decided to set higher standards for myself—that it was going to be different for me. What I saw showed me what I did not want."

Imagine investing $200 in something you love and watching it grow to over $200 million in just ten years. That's exactly what Dan Caldwell and his partners did back in 1997. They had little money but big hopes and dreams—and a love for what many saw as a brutal sport. In their eyes, they envisioned a real opportunity.

MMA, a full-contact combat sport that allows the use of both striking and grappling techniques, draws on a variety of other combat sports and martial arts. In 1993, when it was still illegal in most states, an eight-man tournament with no weight classes and few rules debuted in Denver as the Ultimate Fighting Championship (later renamed UFC 1: The Beginning). The age-old question of which martial arts discipline was the most effective would finally be answered. The answer was "none of the above."

The competitors' fighting styles included boxing, traditional martial arts, and kickboxing—a 440-pound Sumo wrestler even participated. The most unlikely participant shocked the world of combat sports as he won that night, weighing in at only 170 pounds. Brazilian jujitsu artist Royce Gracie easily defeated world-class athletes in other disciplines, achieving most submissions by lying flat on his back, inviting his opponent to go for what looked like an easy victory. Royce then used his legs and arms to maneuver his competitor into positions that few had ever seen or experienced. Royce inflicted pain or restricted breathing to such a degree that each opponent would "tap out," signaling that he was surrendering. A new sport was born—along with a new vocabulary and a new palette of fighting skills. Arm bars, triangles, rear-necked chokes, leg locks, and a host of other techniques were exposed to the mainstream.

Dan Caldwell watched the tournament—and fell in love with the sport. But what separated Dan from so many others who watched that night was that he and his cofounders recognized an opportunity. He remembers, "There was no real brand for this up-and-coming sport." Dan and his partners started TapouT with just a few hundred dollars.

To establish a brand and a unique look, they created individual images and names for themselves: Punkass, Mask, and Skyskrape. Feeling that traditional-style logos were too small, Dan recalls the decision to make a bold logo: "If we are paying these fighters to wear our brand, we needed to make sure everyone would see it." This is how the TapouT logo became a visually no-miss brand. They maxed out their credit cards selling their T-shirts out of their cars, at underground MMA competitions, and at high school jujitsu tournaments.

Dan is proud of their perseverance: "One step at a time, we grew it into a monster of a company. We were doing $100 million when our closest competitor was doing less than a million!" By 2010, Authentic Brands Group LLC acquired TapouT for $200 million.

"Punkass" Mindset

Dan shared valuable wisdom about the battle in your mind as you begin to go for your audacious dream:

People are often constricted by their insecurities. I know I personally battled insecurities all of my life, so I know what it does to you. Insecurities will hold you down—and keep you down—if you let them. I lived in a world where I was just never good enough or smart enough. I never thought I could have what those successful people over on the other side of the tracks had.

When I finally got the courage to attempt something, I was so worried that I was going to fail that I overcompensated in every way. I would have to research everything I could find on whatever subject I was pursuing. I wanted to make sure I did it better and differently and with more imagination than anyone else—because I had to! I would live with it, constantly considering how I could better my idea.

Once I started to have success in different areas, I began to gain confidence and learned to think less about my insecurities. You get this momentum, like a train traveling down the tracks. When the train starts moving, a simple piece of scrap metal on the tracks could stop it, but once it starts to gain momentum, it's virtually unstoppable.

Overcompensating for my personal insecurities has helped me forge ahead in life, blaze trails, and achieve things I never thought possible at one time. When chasing a goal, I have always made one commitment—a "must" that I've always held—to make sure I do something every single day to advance toward my goal. No matter how small, I will never let that day go by without doing at least one thing. I constantly educate myself. If I'm in the gym, driving, or running, I am listening to a book, a podcast, or a YouTube video. I'm finding out those things I don't know—that I need to know. I am listening to other leaders or businessmen who have written books so that I can learn from their mistakes. I take some comfort in knowing that I am outworking my competition!

"Overcompensating for my personal insecurities has helped me forge ahead in life, blaze trails, and achieve things I never thought possible at one time."
—Dan Caldwell

The miles you must run to get to your goal are never easy—in fact, it's probably the most difficult thing you'll ever do. But do you really want to go through life in mediocrity? We are meant to experience life! Pursuing your dreams should not cause you to fear. Rather, the thought of being average should bring you fear, anxiety, and sleepless nights. I think everyone wants their life to be meaningful and to have a purpose. So why not chase that idea, invention, or career that excites your soul? After all, what's the worst that can happen? You'll fail? We all fail! We must fail so that we can learn from those failures. I've had so many failures, I've stopped counting! But my successes far outweigh my failures. Theodore Roosevelt once said, "If he fails, at least he fails while daring greatly. So his place shall never be with those cold and timid souls who know neither victory nor defeat!" We owe ourselves that!

Business success stories come in many forms. Dan is a living example of someone who refused to allow where he began to dictate where he would end up.

Do Not Listen to the Naysayers

Why am I encouraging you to start your own business? Because I was your age and had little going for me when I became an entrepreneur. I proved making the most of what you have can lead to financial independence. As a teenager and through my mid-twenties, I was always in trouble for one thing or another. It seemed that the odds of making something out of my life were a longshot at best. School was not my thing. I never had a grade higher than a C. I ruined every summer vacation for my family because I failed classes so often I had to attend summer school just to get to the next grade. Before I started my own business, I pumped gas, sold vacuums door-to-door, scrubbed bakery floors, and was fired from all sorts of jobs.

Look at all the businesses that started out of a garage. Some are new, and some are old, but all the following share humble beginnings: Amazon, Microsoft, Disney, Apple, Google, Harley-Davidson, Hewlett-Packard, Mattel, Dell, and Nike.

I made my money the old-school way. When I stated my business, I didn't take a salary the first couple of years, so I supported myself by having numerous side jobs, sometimes three at a time. But at the age of twenty-six, with an investment of two grand, I started a small art publishing and distribution company and grew it into an organization that has represented some of the most important and best-known celebrities, business leaders, movie studios, and athletes of the twentieth century. During my early years of business, I was still working as a personal trainer, bartender, and bouncer. Years later, I sold my business to Getty Images for millions.

Others may doubt, asking you, "How can you dare to start your own business? After all, you don't have experience." I didn't either! The only reason I was able to get into college was because I played football and earned a scholarship. My degree is in food science and nutrition. During my business career, we marketed and sold a wide range of high-end collectibles, including art, sunken treasure, meteorites, and fossils. I knew nothing about these items, but I still figured out how to distribute and sell all our products worldwide, both retail and wholesale.

When we manufactured products under license agreements, we were known as the company that created "the crown jewel" of consumer products. So don't let anybody tell you it can't be done. Look at all the businesses that started out in a garage. Some are new, and some are old, but all the following share humble beginnings: Amazon, Microsoft, Disney, Apple, Google, Harley Davidson, Hewlett-Packard, Mattel, Dell, and Nike.

Establish Entrepreneurial Personality Traits

I have worked side by side with many millionaires and have seen, over and over again, what separates these people from the average Jane or Joe. It's not background or who they know or their bank account. So, what is it? It's the way they make decisions, their attitude toward work, and their personality traits, like grit and discipline, that set them on the right course.

If your attitude or work ethic leads you to accept mediocrity, then you have surrendered any hope of excellence. Entrance into the business world has never been easier. Is that a positive for you? Yes. But it also means more competition than ever before. Enthusiasm goes a long way, but you need to be creative and innovative if you want to separate yourself from the pack.

I believe productive attitude, positive mindset, and vision for an organization all start at the top. That means *you* need to set the tone for employees. I ran a very profitable business for more than twenty-five years and have done my fair share of business consulting for all sorts of companies, big and small. I see what they do, both right and wrong. You could have the best product or service in the world, but if you manage incorrectly or set a poor example for your staff or customers, your business can be history before you know it.

> Enthusiasm goes a long way, but you need to be creative and
> innovative if you want to separate yourself from the pack.

According to the Small Business Association (SBA), 30 percent of new businesses fail during the first two years of being open, 50 percent during the first five years, and 66 percent during the first ten.[82] A business can fall short of its goals for many reasons: inability to create a profitable business model, price/value ratio that has not been proven within the marketplace, failure to establish a successful marketing/advertising program, lack of unique offerings compared to competition, inadequate funding, shortcomings in leadership's ability to communicate a clear, well-thought-out vision, and breakdown in follow-through.

Can you defy the odds? Absolutely. How? Become a master motivator to yourself, employees, and clients. Focus on your passion, not your fears. Become a great listener. Ask questions as often as possible. (Ask once and that information is yours forever.) Don't react emotionally to any situation; rather, calmly evaluate before your respond. Become a people person. If you are an introvert, learn to network and communicate effectively in business situations.

During an interview, I was once asked what I did as a CEO. Without thinking, I said, "I make decisions." Yes, you, as CEO, will have many responsibilities, but if you can't make decisions, you'll go nowhere fast. What is the best approach to decision-making? First, gather important and relevant information. Then, discuss options and alternatives with those you trust and respect, including mentors and staff members.

When I am not sure about a decision, I often ask myself, "Can I live with the worst-case scenario?" If the answer is no, then I won't go

---

82 "Top 6 Reasons New Businesses Fail," Investopedia, https://www.investopedia.com/slide-show/top-6-reasons-new-businesses-fail/.

forward. If the answer is yes, most likely I can live with a bad outcome and I will move forward. Putting off a decision for too long can slow down your company's growth and create confusion among your staff.

So, have an attitude that says, "Go for the no." Hockey great Wayne Gretzky said, "You miss 100 percent of the shoots you don't take." You will sleep better at night knowing that you went after something, rather than endless pondering, which dilutes action. For me, better to get turned down or rejected than to fail to pursue a worthy cause. Strive for excellence, not perfection. If you wait to have every tiny detail in place to begin, you're waiting too long. You need to become a decision maker and a well-disciplined multitasker. As a successful CEO, you will make many decisions each day. Somewhere down the line, if you realize you were wrong, don't worry; just fix it and move on.

Be accountable for your company's success. Yes, you will need help, but at the end of the day, it's your company, and it's your responsibly to make it work. Excuses are always available and convenient. As a business owner, you may not have the luxury of letting somebody else figure it out. If you have a problem, solve it. This is how you get to the next level. Whatever business you decide to explore, you need to become an expert within your chosen industry. This takes time and research, but without question, it's mandatory for long-term success and needs to be a priority.

Be accountable for your company's success . . . Even though you are young, you can be a great leader.

Even though you are young, you can be a great leader. Others will be watching to see how you handle the various demands of running a business. One day, I would clean a toilet bowl, but the next day, I would cut a $1 million deal. That can-do attitude—no matter the task—will spread throughout your organization and serve you well. You never want employees to think, "Well, if the boss doesn't work hard, why should I?"

Great leadership will empower your staff to succeed. It will set the expectation that they work together as a team for a common cause. If you want others to get on board with your vision, you need to be well spoken and communicate a clear and focused plan. Leadership is being an inspiration to others, the cheerleader who will help all reach their full potential. Leadership is not imposing your will on others. A true leader earns respect with their actions and fosters the loyalty needed for the whole enterprise to prosper.

Please understand, before your concept crowns you with great success, you will have plenty of adversity and setbacks. Any successful entrepreneur will tell you they didn't get every deal or every sale. But they will also tell you they used setbacks as fuel to keep moving forward.

Old-School Grit: Mark Cuban

Business icon and entrepreneur Mark Cuban got right to the point during our interview. Mark went from bartender to billionaire to NBA team owner and happens to be the wealthiest cast member on the Emmy Award-winning show *Shark Tank*. Talk about a gritty attitude. Mark simply has no give-up and losing is not within his vocabulary.

"The power to achieve success lies within you. Sweat equity is the best equity—and everyone has a bank full of it. They just have to choose to use it."
—Mark Cuban

Mark passionately shared insight I'd like to pass along to you:

I want to kick the ass of the people I am competing with, and that always motivates me to push myself to know as much as I can about my business and puts me in a position to create new ideas. Nothing will come easy . . . hard work is something everyone talks about but rarely does . . . if you do something you love, then working hard is easy. If you can work hard enough to be really, really good at something—anything—you can usually find a way to reach your goals. The power to achieve success lies within you; sweat equity is the best equity—and everyone has a bank full of it. They just have to choose to use it.

Entrepreneurial Education

Fact is, creating a product or service is not that hard. We all have ideas. The hard part comes when you try to sell a large volume of what you've created. Truth be told, starting your own business can be both stressful and exhilarating at the same time. Remember, your primary job as CEO is to make decisions. But if you are not well informed, then you will likely make bad decisions. The knowledge you possess is a valuable commodity, and entrepreneurship is a skill that can be learned—if you're willing to put in the hours to learn. But before you invest your time or money and before you raise capital for your business venture, I strongly suggest taking a few business courses. The more well informed you are, the more likely your startup is to prosper. Knowledge is true power.

Digital courses on entrepreneurship are available, on both online platforms and through campuses around the world. These types of courses now form a multibillion-dollar industry. Accessing the knowledge of brilliant business minds has never been easier. Professors from Harvard, Stanford, The University of Chicago, or MIT are only a click away. If you don't have the funds or time to take on a full-time schedule, just YouTube away for an abundance of knowledge.

I happen to like Warren Buffet. He started his company Berkshire Hathaway decades ago and is now worth in excess of $85 billion. I have gained valuable insight and wisdom about investing and business from Mr. Buffet. Did I pay a dime? No. It was and still is available online: https://buffett.cnbc.com/. You can view over one hundred and thirty hours of free, searchable videos dating back twenty-five years. The topics are endless.

What subject matter do you need more information on? Sales, negotiation, leadership, basic bookkeeping and accounting, marketing/advertising, or small business management? How about a class that focuses on your business goals? What will your take-aways be? Start by learning best practices in the industry you are in, and over time, you'll develop your own.

Now, let me ask you a question. If for three months you put off starting your business and used that time to learn relevant business knowledge, how much better would your chances of succeeding be? I rest my case. Take a few business courses!

Next, seek out a mentor. You will find few things as valuable as having an experienced and trusted mentor in your corner. Their knowledge, advice, motivation, resources, and emotional support can help you get to your next level. When you meet, have pen and pad or iPad in hand and be prepared to ask specific questions about areas of your business that need improvement. You would be surprised, but many of the most brilliant business minds still have mentors and are still on the lookout to learn as much as they can. Why? Because what they learn will make them more money.

You will find few things as valuable as having an experienced and trusted mentor in your corner.

Creative, Innovative, and Proactive

Do you have to be creative and innovative to succeed in business? Yes, but all too often, people with truly fantastic ideas lack the discipline and confidence to proactively move their solutions or concepts past the beginning stages. Being proactive—that is, charging forward with boldness—can separate you from the pack.

I've tried to convey a constant theme throughout this book: when you have something you desire, you must be accountable for your own success; you must be proactive. You can be the smarter guy or girl, be better funded, or have the greatest connections, but in business, if you are not proactive, you will fail.

Remember, others are going after the same things you are going after. If they are more aggressive, more determined, and more proactive, you will be marginalized and left in the dust. You need to be honest with yourself. If you don't have a driven mindset, and don't see yourself growing bolder, then running a business is not for you.

So, how do you start? How do you take those first steps? Get out there and network. Have an open-minded attitude, convey a friendly demeanor, and engage in conversations. If you're not talking to others in your industry, you're missing out. Over time, you will form business connections, share information, and help each other succeed. So, be proactive in attending seminars, conferences, or industry trade shows. Enthusiastically watch webinars. My attitude toward learning opportunities was (and still is), even if I only learn one new skill or technique, it's a home run.

If other business owners are more aggressive, more determined, and more proactive, you will be marginalized and left in the dust.

Feel-Good Story: *Family Guy* Creator Seth MacFarlane

During my career as CEO of a company selling art, I was able to do business with many legends, including three-time Emmy winner Seth MacFarlane, creator of *Family Guy.* How did Seth make it to the top of his field? By using his creativity and innovation and employing an intense, proactive mindset.

I first met *Family Guy* creator Seth MacFarlane when he was only twenty-four years old. He was television's youngest executive producer, and *Family Guy* was still in its infancy. Looking back, I'm still amazed that my company had the opportunity to do the first in-person art-signing gallery event through the Fox Animation Art Program. Talk about being proactive! Getting Seth to fly from California to New York was no easy task.

Seth's first job earned him five dollars a week for his comic strip *Walter Crouton* for the *Kent Good Times Dispatch.* Soon after he graduated from the Rhode Island School of Design, where he studied animation, Seth joined the legendary animation studio Hanna-Barbera. He was still working with Hanna-Barbera when he had the idea for *Family Guy* and confidently approached the Fox Broadcasting Company. They told Seth, "If you can do a pilot for us for, like, $50,000, we'll give you a shot at a series." (Typically, costs to produce a half-hour episode for a primetime animated show can exceed $1 million.) Many would have been intimidated and walked away from the opportunity. Seth had a choice to make: have the can't-do attitude or have a proactive, can-do attitude.

Seth told me about this period, "Obviously, I said, 'Yeah, I'll do it,' not knowing whether I could or not. I spent about six months with no sleep and no life—just drawing like crazy in my kitchen and doing this pilot." At the end of the six months, Seth presented the show to Fox executives, and they loved it. They ordered thirteen episodes of

Family Guy. Seth's style, talent, innovation, and dedication resulted in his becoming television's youngest executive producer.

The *Family Guy* franchise is now a billion-dollar-plus industry, and Seth continues to be one of the highest-paid television writers, having signed a deal worth over $100 million. Seth still enjoys being the voice of four characters from Quahog, Rhode Island: Peter, Stewie, and Brian Griffin and Glenn Quagmire. Let Seth's proactive mindset, innovation, and commitment to his dream be an inspiration to you to be the very best you can.

While it's true that being proactive can pay off, please understand that being proactive is not always about getting "the big deal." Rather, it's about the little things that need to get done on a daily basis for your business to survive and prosper: tedious paperwork; annoying calls; the boring, long drive to meetings; and the repetitive, endless tasks only you can do. The list of thankless jobs you will have as a CEO—especially in the beginning as you grow your organization—is long but necessary.

Appreciation Is a Fundamental Human Need

How you treat others in the world of business could affect your entire career. Never forget the golden rule: treat employees the way you would like to be treated. Long ago, I learned one of the most important human emotions is to feel appreciated. Showing appreciation to your employees and clients costs nothing, yet the goodwill generated is priceless.

Your business etiquette and the way you communicate to your staff, vendors, and associates will cause others to judge you either affectionately or harshly. In running my business, I've hired hundreds of people, including sales personnel, secretaries, shipping clerks, middle management, accountants, and executives. I made million-dollar deals and plenty of smaller deals. I learned many things about people and their emotions. I can say with certainty that making people feel appreciated is essential.

Appreciation is a fundamental human need. We all want validation of our efforts. To me, it's a basic rule: make others feel good about their work and say thank you as often as possible. When you have employees and others in your business circle who are happy with the way they are treated, you enjoy increased loyalty to your company. Their confidence, motivation, and self-esteem will also increase, which leads to a more productive employee, one who will do their best to help you succeed. It's amazing how far a simple thank-you letter, a one-on-one sit-down, or an acknowledgment in front of others can go. By the way, the cost to you in dollars is zero. All that's required is kind words and a smile on your face, but the return is invaluable.

You are the leader of your company culture, and what they see you do, they will do. Lead by example. Inspire all you come in contact with. Show empathy; take the high road; admit and fix mistakes. If you are committed to honesty and integrity, you will attract good people into your world.

Prepare to be an effective communicator. State your rules and mission clearly. Always be prepared to answer questions and provide reasons for your decisions. Make sure you provide basic social comfort, creating an environment where others feel secure and respected in the workplace. If there's a bully in the house, get rid of them. Set the tone for a productive and successful environment. Share credit for success with everyone.

More often than not, I recommend you hire for attitude not aptitude. Most people with a good attitude can be trained in a variety of areas. If you are looking for your staff to work as a team with a common mindset of "we can get it done," then hire people who are focused on the positive. If you have someone in your organization who always seems to point out what's going wrong, their outlook will likely drag others down. Foster a culture of collaboration by planning team-building events; they really do work well for morale.

Customer Service

Your goal must be to become a well-oiled machine with policies and protocols in place. This is particularly crucial when things don't go as planned. Your clients and consumers will have high standards and expectations of what they expect from your organization. With just a click of a button, a customer can post a devastating review of your company. Train your staff to be friendly and patient when speaking with an unhappy client. Teach them to listen empathetically and let the customer vent before offering a solution.

It's perfectly fine to apologize, take the high road, and offer refunds if you can't resolve the issue. Don't argue; be respectful. If you need to look into what happened and you don't have all the answers for the customer while speaking with them, it's fine to say you need to look into the situation further, but you should make every effort to get back to the disgruntled client the same day. Going into a sale, if you think you're heading down the path with a problem customer, you'll be better off saying no thank you to the sale. The money is not worth it. Best to avoid people looking for a fight or to cause problems.

Create a Business Flowchart

If you want your staff to be on the same page, create a flowchart. What will this do? It will reduce uncertainty concerning who does what and when. It may also expose potential problems and issues. A flowchart should be simple and easy to follow. Track the step-by-step process from the time an order comes in until your product or service is in the client's hands. You may need to create a flowchart for each division of your company, like marketing, production, customer service, accounting, shipping, human resources, and so on.

This may sound like a lot of work, but it's well worth the time and effort. If you won't or can't put your processes in a diagram form, you're making a mistake. Having a set of activities that accomplish a specific organizational goal puts all your employees on the same page. You can analyze the diagram with other staff members to pinpoint the bugs and inefficiencies slowing your company down. Use your flowchart to establish an open dialogue with the goal to make your organization more effective and the customer's experience more pleasurable.

Training

Training is an essential part of any business, but keep your sessions short and to the point. Get people involved; let your workforce offer input on what should be included in training modules. Role play works wonders for salespeople and other staff members who engage directly with your clients. Practice what their response should be to customer objections, questions about product details, and complaints. Anything employees deal with over and over on a daily basis will make for a good role play.

Make sure you are prepared to offer the training. Have an agenda and explain each point in a way all can understand. Keep an open mind and be ready to answer questions. Remember, your employees are in the trenches and can give you a firsthand account of what's going right and wrong—if you'll listen. As you develop new insight, evolve your training accordingly.

A Word About Salespeople

Chances are, when you start your first business, you will be the biggest advocate and cheerleader of your product or service. As the founder, you are rightfully concerned about how much revenue you generate and how many sales have been made. With growth, you will likely bring salespeople onboard.

From experience, I have some thoughts on how you should treat your salespeople. Besides hiring and training hundreds of salespeople over my career as a business owner, I have also worked as a sales consultant to many companies. Too often, salespeople are not treated with the respect they deserve. I see this contributing to the resentment others in the company have against salespeople.

Why would other employees resent the sales team? Unfortunately, salespeople are notorious for being spoiled, asking for too much, and being an overall pain in the neck. I've witnessed, time and time again, administration or others in the organization not liking a sales member personally. So they ask, "Why do we put up with them? If it was up to me, I would get rid of them." Really? The sales team brings money into the business. So what if their personality isn't what appeals to you? You didn't hire them because of their pleasantries; you hired them to produce revenue.

I can't tell you how many times I've had issues with my salespeople, but I always go to the greatest extent to resolve any conflicts. Why? Because at the end of the month when the bills are due, you pay expenses with the money your sales team brought in. You can have the greatest product or service in the world but if you don't have others advocating and selling on your behalf, the growth of your company will be limited.

Who falls into the category of sales? Anybody who works for you and produces direct revenue or sales results. This includes those who generate service fees, advertising sales, or commissions. It's not the paper pushers, accountants, or those who answer the phone. Keep proper perspective and remember all salespeople bring to the company. And, they must deal with constant rejection. Sales associates will get many more nos than yeses, and that alone can drive a sane person crazy. So, be kind, understanding, and respectful as you interact with this population.

To keep them motivated, I suggest awarding a quarterly bonus (in addition to salary) and set up an appealing commission plan. Good salespeople set goals for themselves. Few things motivate salespeople more than a nice check at the end of the month. As a sidenote, remember that you are responsible for the actions of your staff. Keep a keen eye out for salespeople who push the limit. If they lie or mislead clients, show them the door.

How to Choose a Business

The pathway to starting your own business begins with your imagination, creativity, dedication, desire, and talents. It will require thinking differently than others, seeing possibility where others only see problems. Keep in mind, your idea is just an idea if you can't figure out a way to monetize it. You may not be able to solve all the world's problems, but you can find your niche and help others in that space while creating an ongoing business.

Let's first make sure you understand what makes a successful business. Here's my simple equation for a successful business: business revenue (money generated through your company) is greater than all expenses (cost to run your company, salaries, inventory, rent, insurance, etc.). If you can keep that one goal in mind, you are heading in the right direction.

Nothing was ever invented, only discovered.

In all of history, nothing was ever invented, only discovered. That truth should motivate you to think outside the box and dare to ask questions others think are unsolvable. The founder of Apple, Steve Jobs, brought the iPhone to market, and it has changed life as we know it. However, all the components to create a smartphone have been on the earth for millions of years. It took Steve and his team to put the components together to "invent" the device. The same holds true for any product or service you can think of. It's up to you to use your mind to discover the next big thing.

Ask yourself the following questions about your product or service:

- What problem or struggle am I solving?
- Is there a void in the marketplace I can fill?
- What are the benefits to the consumer?
- How can I improve on what already exists?
- What is unique about my offer?
- Do I have the skill set to make it happen?
- What funds will I need to create my vision?
- How will I support myself until I make a profit?
- Do I have the time to give 100 percent effort?
- Are those close to me supportive?
- Am I risking too much? Can I survive and move on if it doesn't work?
- Should I test run my concept part-time before quitting my job?
- Am I passionate enough to maintain my discipline and dedication?
- What can I do better than the competition?
- Is there a niche I can fill?
- How will I build trust with my customer?

One of the best ways to decide what type of business you may want is to attend a trade show, speak with a business broker, or visit a franchise event. Chances are, you won't buy a franchise but walking the aisles can be business education on steroids. Who could you possibly speak with? Perhaps management teams from McDonald's, 7-Eleven, KFC, or Subway? Yes, but to get into those franchises would certainly be a big chuck of change. So, how about FIT4MOM, Chem-Dry, Mosquito Squad, Pinspiration, or Jazzercise? These offer franchise fees ranging from only $1,250-$25,000.

We have already addressed the importance of being proactive. So you know that just walking around a trade show is not good enough.

You need to get into as many conversations as you can. To sell a franchise, the company must give potential buyers full disclosure. This means company representatives will tell you who their competition is, what profit margin they work on, how they market, what they do differently from their competitors, and a host of other valuable business information. I am certainly not saying all franchises are great businesses, but they have worked out all the kinks you might face as a startup. So, discussing their best practices should prove very educational as you make your own decisions. Who knows? Maybe something in your mind will spark and you will be inspired to do what Ralph Waldo Emerson once said: "Build a better mousetrap, and the world will beat a path to your door."

Don't over complicate things. Sometimes the simplest ideas are the best ideas. Certainly, if you have a new concept or idea, run with it. If you have the next $1 billion app, make it happen! If you think you can be a huge social media influencer, do it. Or just click on Google and find many potential business ideas: bicycle repair, boat cleaning, chimney cleaning service, computer repair, personal wellness, graphic design, social media management, marketing copywriter, dating consultant, college admissions essay editor, WordPress or website consultant, or virtual assistant services.

How about turning your hobby into a business? You could teach art, piano, voice lessons, acting, yoga, cooking, photography, writing, or carpentry. You could offer specialized sports coaching. If you are looking to start a business that will be attractive to millennials, keep in mind that positive social impact should be part of its appeal. You can create products or services to sell to the wholesale market or directly to the consumer. Wholesale is selling your product, usually in larger quantities, to other companies who will then offer them to consumers.

How about talking over your options with friends and family? Have a brainstorming session. Discuss what's needed in today's ever-changing society: What could the world use today? What could be done better? What are people complaining about that needs improvement?

Look at the technology you have at the tip of your fingers: 3-D printers, social media, group financing, and so much more. Get familiar with Moore's Law, a computing term which originated around 1970; the simplified version of this law states that processor speeds, or overall processing power for computers, will double every two years.[83] What does that mean for you? Technology will continue to advance, giving you more options and opportunities.[84]

Have you ever heard the phrase "creative destruction"? Creative destruction is a concept in economics, most readily identified with the Austrian-American economist Joseph Schumpeter who derived it from the work of Karl Marx and popularized it as a theory of economic innovation and the business cycle. According to Schumpeter, the "process of industrial mutation incessantly revolutionizes the economic structure from within, incessantly destroying the old one, incessantly creating a new one."[85] This means individuals throughout history have created better products or services that eventually become the dominant product or service. So how about trying to identity an industry or product that is prime for improvement or disruption? If it's been done thousands of times in the past, then why can't you do the same?

Make sure to do your due diligence, whether you acquire an existing business or start your own business from scratch. Due diligence is an investigation and analysis of a business. If it's a company or franchise you want to acquire, become very familiar with how the business operates. Hire an accountant to audit all the financial records and review them

---

83   Moore's Law," Investopedia, April 20, 2019, https://www.investopedia.com/terms/m/mooreslaw.asp.

84   "Creative Destruction," Investopedia, April 15, 2019, https://www.investopedia.com/terms/c/creativedestruction.asp.

85   Margaret Rouse, "Creative Destruction," WhatIs.com, July 2013, https://whatis.techtarget.com/definition/creative-destruction.

with you. Have a thorough understanding of the cost of goods, profit margin, payroll taxes inventory, physical assets, short-term and long-term obligations, and liabilities. Has the company paid their taxes? A qualified accountant can walk you through all the numbers.

In addition, hire a lawyer to review leases, permits, and contracts. A lawyer may recommend you buy the assets of the company and not the legal organization itself. This can protect you if, later on, you discover something was not disclosed. Don't hire an accountant or lawyer who intimidates you. You should be comfortable asking lots of questions. Don't just go to a family friend who *thinks* they know business. In the short run, it will be less money, but in the long run, you could be involving yourself in something you will regret. Pay a qualified accountant and lawyer to save yourself future headaches.

If your vision is to start your company from the ground up, the same amount of due diligence is required. In this instance, turn the spotlight on the industry you are interested in. Familiarize yourself with the size of the market and define who your competition will be. Do your best to see if it will be a viable business. Find the cost of goods and what others are selling the product/service for. Before you put money into your venture, outline how you will structure your business and all associated cost. Put in the hard work of research before risking capital.

Feel-Good Story: My First Business

I started a little business when I was only seventeen years old. I loved the beach but hated having to walk back to the boardwalk to buy a drink. Once in a while, I saw guys walk around closer to shore with coolers, yelling out, "Cold soda here! Get your cold soda here!" I decided to do a little investigation and spoke to some of these individuals. I learned they were making pretty good money, about $100 to $200 a day. Even then, I was business savvy. I knew I had to evaluate the market to see what I could do differently, how I could make it better and earn more.

I saw soda being sold but realized a full cooler of soda cans would be heavy and bulky. Ice cream would be a hit, but it melted quickly in the hot sun. Fruit cups would go bad if they were not sold fast. So, I went to my local supermarket and noticed little plastic containers of fruit juice. They were light and would last indefinitely—an improvement on the other options I'd considered. The price was also right. The grocer was selling seven juices for one dollar, and I could fit about fifty in my cooler.

Next thing you know, I was selling the drinks on the beach for one dollar each. Soon, I had to bring in a friend to help me out. We were both football players who could work all day carrying the coolers around the beach. Of course, trouble always followed me around. One day my friend and I found ourselves surrounded by five or six tough guys trying to intimidate us. They said there was a "union" and we couldn't sell on their beach.

Now I knew just as well as they did that *nobody* was supposed to be selling drinks on the beach, so there was no union. No permits were issued, and if the cops saw us, we were always chased off the beach. This little gang picked the wrong guys to mess with. We had a little brawl, and by the time it was done, they were a mess. As the fight ended, they said they wanted us to stay but asked if we would join their "union" and help kick others off the beach. Because I am a capitalist and believe in competition, we said no thanks.

How to Raise Capital

First things first: if you are not 100 percent committed to your business, then don't ask others for money. Even if you are committed, bear in mind that while many successful businesses have been established by raising capital through friends and family, many more relationships have been ruined. Unfortunately, most businesses will fail; therefore, people you care about will lose their investment. Even if you are profitable, crazy things happen. Emotions get involved and somebody always feels mistreated or shortchanged. If you do raise funds from friends or family or any other entity, don't go overboard with your projected income. Your credibility is on the line. Make sure you have a written agreement—prepared by a lawyer—that all understand. It's not a perfect solution, but a clear agreement should help protect all those involved.

Prepare your business plan. You can find templates online to get started. A visit to the US Small Business Administration (SBA) website may also help: https://www.sba.gov/. Work with a mentor and/or an accountant to develop your plan, which should include the following: an overview of the business you want to start (executive summary); a description of who you are and of those you intend to bring into the organization (organization management); an assessment of the market and of your competitive advantage (market analysis); important selling points (sales strategies); and funding requirements/financial projections.

One great way to raise money without having to give a large percentage away is to show potential investors your "proof of concept." Proof of concept shows evidence, typically derived from a pilot project, that demonstrates your concept or business idea is attainable.[86] In other words, you create a prototype or sample of your vision, you bring to it market, and hopefully create sales. This is easier than it sounds with today's technology.

Showing an investor you are able to execute your idea and create even a modest revenue stream will do wonders when asking for money. If the investor believes you will be able to successfully scale the business (grow or expand it in a proportional and usually profitable way), you should have little problem raising capital. For example, if you think you have a clothing line that will sell, create a few samples and offer them on social media, Shopify, Etsy, or eBay. Marketing and advertising has

---

86   Sean Murphy, "Proof of Concept vs Pilot," Nexus, February 10, 2014, http://www.nexusnet.com.au/2014/02/10/proof-of-concept-vs-pilot-program/.

never been easier with Google AdWords, Facebook, Twitter, LinkedIn, Pinterest ads, and Instagram.

Small Business Administration (SBA) loans are one of the best ways to raise capital for your small business. Because they are guaranteed by a federal agency, banks and lenders can offer them with flexible terms and low interest rates. The SBA can guarantee up to 85 percent of loans of $150,000 or less and 75 percent of loans greater than $150,000. SBA Veterans Advantage loans offer even better terms for those who have served in the military. For minorities, SBA microloans offer up to $50,000 through nonprofit organizations. Interest rates and terms of repayment are flexible.

Crowdfunding is another option. Over $334 billion was raised worldwide by crowdfunding.[87] This means you fund your project or venture by raising small amounts of money from a large number of people. Some of the largest crowdfunding platforms include Indiegogo, Kickstarter, and GoFundMe.

How about sweat equity? If you can find someone to invest in your expertise, your "investment" will not be money but your knowledge and hard work that leads to business ownership. As an example, let's say you're a great chef but you don't have the funds to open up your own restaurant. Your goal would be to find an investor who would use their own funds to open up the restaurant and pay the overhead and bills. Your job as a sweat equity participant would be to manage the kitchen with little or no compensation (pay). You would enter into an agreement with the investor. As the restaurant produces revenue and makes money, the time and effort you spent as the chef would, in turn, give you partial ownership of the establishment.

---

87 "Crowdfunding," *Wikipedia*, last updated August 5, 2019, https://en.wikipedia. org/wiki/Crowdfunding.

Then there's always an initial public offering (IPO). This refers to the process of offering shares of your private corporation to the public in a new stock issuance. Public share issuance allows a company to raise capital from public investors. However, much is involved going public. I would suggest you seek advice from an investment banker who can evaluate if it's feasible and in your best interest to take your company public with an IPO. He can get you up to speed on the process, due diligence, pricing, regulations, and documentation needed.[88]

For me, self-finance was the way to go. I never felt comfortable asking others for money. For the first two years, as I grew my business and paid others' salaries, I didn't take any compensation. What did I do? I worked during the day and was a bouncer/ bartender at night. On the weekends or early mornings, I worked as a personal trainer. Where there's a will, there's a way. Bouncing may not be your cup of tea, but when you're determined, you can always find a way to make money.

However you decide to finance your business, make sure to present yourself as a professional. Get rid of the T-shirts and dress for success. It could be the difference between somebody giving you a chance versus walking away.

You also need to hone your communication skills. Compose a clear pitch about your vision and objectives. Be concise; don't go on and on. Get to the point. Be compelling and enthusiastic. Consolidate what you have in your business plan and present it to your audience. Make it easy for people to understand your key points. Don't overdo it. In general, people with money have heard it all before and will see through any BS. Be ready to answer any and all questions. Investors are "buying" into you just as much as your idea. Prepare, prepare, and prepare some more.

---

88 "What Is the IPO Process?" Corporate Finance Institute, https://corporatefinanceinstitute.com/resources/knowledge/finance/ipo-process/.

Build a Brand

Prioritize and construct a feasible timeline for each step. Your working plan should outline the following: financial and other resources required; pricing strategy; what makes you different from your competition; a plan for product or service development; and a marketing and advertising strategy.

Part of your ongoing task is to create a company brand. Your logo is important, but it is not your brand. *The Dictionary of Brand* defines brand as "a person's perception of a product, service, experience, or organization."[89] Jeff Bezos, founder and CEO of Amazon, says, "Your brand is what other people say about you when you're not in the room."[90] Your customer holds the key to your success. Deliver on your promises and make sure your company's behavior and objectives are sending the message by which you want to be judged. You won't be able to make everybody happy, but take the right steps to come as close as you can.

Become the expert in your field. To help with this, blog consistently and include photography and video. Make sure what you write is relevant to your topic. An additional benefit will be a higher ranking with Google. Your blog doesn't have to be high tech, but it needs to be authentic and educational, delivering to your current and potential clients what they are looking for. Don't make what you post or blog all about selling your product; let that be an afterthought. Make it fun and informative.[91]

---

89   Josh Ritchie, "Why Your Brand Is More Than Just a Visual Identity," LinkedIn Marketing Soutions Blog, July 31, 2018, https://business.linkedin.com/ marketing-solutions/blog/linkedin-b2b-marketing/2018/why-your-brand-is-more-than-just-a-visual-identity.

90   "Your Brand Is What Other People Say About You When You're Not in the Room," Marketing & Creative Handbook, http://home.mch.co.uk/your-brand-is-what-people-say-about-you-when-youre-not-in-the-room.shtml.

91   "Google Loves Video: How to Rank Higher on Google," Moovly, https://www. moovly.com/blog/google-loves-video-how-to-rank-higher-on-google-video-maker.

Educate yourself on how to market and advertise your business. These days, it's fairly simple. You can adjust your ad campaign as much as needed and turn your advertising on and off with a click of a button. Videos on how to start advertising and manage your campaigns, supplied by Instagram, Facebook, and other social media platforms, are easy to find online. You will learn how to target your perceived audience: gender, age, hobby, education, zip code, and so much more. Install analytics as this will give you valuable feedback. It's free and will give you customized detailed reports, statistics, and insights about your campaign.[92]

Become the expert in your field . . . blog . . . educate yourself about how to market and advertise your business.

Remain disciplined and stay loyal to the strategy and system you develop to grow your organization. Become a great entrepreneur by making adjustments when needed but without losing your forward momentum.

Reducing Risk

Reality check. Bad things do happen to good people and good businesses. I would strongly suggest that you don't take shortcuts. Work with professional advisors (lawyers, accountants, mentors) to make sure you lay the proper foundation for a profitable business that complies with necessary standards.

---

92   Dinesh Thakur, "10 Good Reasons Why You Should Use Google Analytics," A Medium Corporation, June 20, 2017, https://medium.com/@dineshsem/10-good-reasons-why-you-should-use-google-analytics-699f10194834.

Don't get overwhelmed or intimidated. Just because you've never run a business before, that doesn't mean you can't get it all in place. Take one step at a time, and you will get to where you want to be. With many of these administrative matters, it will be a one-time event; once the hassle of setting up the system has passed, it will seem doable. Other items, such as insurance, taxes, etc., can be scheduled for payment—set it up and then forget about it.

I have seen people with great ideas who never get started because of their insecurity and self-doubt. Don't be that person. Educate yourself and get up to speed. After all, millions of new businesses get started each year. If they can do it, so can you!

Incorporate your business by establishing a limited liability company (LLC). You can do this online through your secretary of state's office. Taking time for this step is an important part of protecting your personal assets. Generally speaking, if something happens in your business and you are sued, as long as you haven't committed fraud, what you own personally should be secure. Anything owned by the business would be at risk. An exception would be taxes owed.

It's a good idea to speak to your accountant about what type of corporation would be appropriate for your organization (LLC vs S Corp vs C Corp, for example). Many new entrepreneurs choose to incorporate as a limited liability company (LLC). Whatever you decide, just be sure not to mix your personal funds with your business funds. Don't pay your personal bills through your business account. This could expose you to penalties and tax consequences that will be hard to deal with.

Acquire a Federal Tax Identification Number. This will establish your business as a separate legal entity. This is also known as an Employer Identification Number (EIN). The IRS will provide this. Pick a name out for your company. Then do a search to make sure it hasn't been trademarked. Again, the secretary of state website in the state where you live will be the place to go to test the availability of the name you have in mind.

Make some calls and find out which business permits and licenses are required for your geographic area and business type. Familiarize yourself with local laws, rules, and guidelines concerning compliance. Go to the Federal Trade Commission website to better understand consumer protection laws.

Sit with your accountant to understand employee laws, rules regarding wages and hours, self-employment taxes, unemployment insurance, federal and state payroll, and withholding taxes. Unless you have a background in accounting, I suggest you have a bookkeeper or accountant handle this area. Plenty of software is on the market to get you organized. Filing correct paperwork and taxes should be a priority. In addition, find out how long you need to keep your backup paperwork for the taxes you filed. Talk with a business insurance agent. Discuss your needs regarding general liability insurance, property Insurance, professional liability insurance, and worker's compensation. No one solution works for every person or every business, so seek out a well-respected professional to gain the best advice.

Have high standards for your product or service. In the long run, these aspirations will serve you well. Be aware that you will be responsible not only for your actions but for those of your staff as well. Yes, you, as the CEO, are ultimately culpable for those who work for you. Make sure all employees understand and follow the rules. Frequently perform quality control tests. Keep good records.

Don't be cash poor and inventory rich. I've seen it over and over, companies spending too much in inventory. Put controls in place and then maintain discipline. What good is all your inventory if you can't pay your bills? Yes, you get a discount for buying larger quantities of items, but is it really worth it? Project what you will sell over a time period and limit yourself to prebuying that much inventory. If you run out, in most cases, additional inventory can always be bought.

Sounds basic, but make sure you have a healthy profit margin in place. If you're only producing revenues and not a profit, why bother? It will be a constant struggle both financially and emotionally. To better understand what your profit margin is, first find your gross profit. This is the difference between the revenue (money generated) and the cost. To find the profit margin, divide gross profit by the revenue. To calculate the margin percentage, multiply the result by one hundred. So, if you sell an item for one hundred dollars and the cost is forty dollars, your profit margin is 60 percent.

Strive to have a healthy bank account with little debt. Always negotiate prices when you can. Over the years, I have saved hundreds of thousands of dollars just because I told (asked) a vendor that they needed to provide me with a better price. For me, simply asking and explaining why I needed a lower cost resulted in a 90 percent success rate. Do the same and profits will come.

Remember the story of Sisyphus in Greek mythology? He pushed the same boulder up a hill, day after day, only to watch it roll back down; his efforts were fruitless, yet he couldn't stop. Sometimes passion and enthusiasm aren't enough. I have seen people lose tons of money because they thought their concept was good but the marketplace didn't agree—but they couldn't admit defeat. Of course, other factors, including execution of plan, unprofitable business model, poor leadership, and lack of funds, can also come into play. But when it's clear your business won't work and you're just doing the same things over and over without progress, learn to cut your losses. We've all heard many stories of people not succeeding in one business and later succeeding in another. So, know how to admit it when one opportunity ends. Another could be ready to begin!

Don't be the stubborn person who will not give up. Don't be the person who borrows money from family or friends that can't be paid back. Don't be the person who puts up their personal assets (house) as collateral and loses it because they wouldn't let the dream die. You may be sad for a while, but when forward motion just won't come, shut down operations, dust yourself off, and get ready for the next venture.

Adapting to Change

Learn to be flexible. More often than not, you will have to adapt—or at least adjust—to change. Consumers can be finicky. One day they may be loyal to your brand, but the next day you're old news. Your offerings can go from hot to not. Don't take it personally. As an entrepreneur, you need to develop mental toughness. Your mindset needs to be, if there's a problem, there's a solution. This is why, if you can successfully guide your company through rough seas, the financial payoff can be big. Always be on the lookout for the latest trends in the market. Be aware what others in your industry are up to. Move quickly to test new products and services. Embrace technology. Measuring your results with analytics will give you the ability to increase or decrease your advertising expenditures.

Talk to your customers; get their feedback. Send out surveys. Have both entry-level price points and high-end price points, for those who "want the best," in your product mix. Test multiple products and services on a small scale. If they work, expand on the success. If they fail, walk away and be happy you found out early on.

I was in the collectibles business for over twenty-five years. We started off selling animation art. When the big movie studios flooded the market with too much product, we moved on to classic rock art. We developed a nice clientele of people who enjoyed collecting many things. When business was a little slow with the art, we offered our customers sunken treasure artifacts, fossils, and meteorites. When we first started advertising, we had success with newspaper ads. When we stopped getting the response we wanted, we went to radio and TV. When the internet came into play, we began advertising on social media. Remember: be flexible.

If we didn't adjust our product line and advertising, over time, the business would have stagnated and died. Truth be told, it takes a special person to run a company and weather the changes. When things are good, most people can step in and claim victory. It's when the business is teetering between life and death that the true visionary and entrepreneur shines.

When things are good, most people can step in and claim victory. It's when the business is teetering between life and death that the true visionary and entrepreneur shines.

Exit Strategy

So, what happens if you create a profitable business? The obvious answer is, you will earn an income and have pride and joy in what you have done. But let's look at other answers too. You could sell your business. The average selling price ranges from two to six times EBIT. EBIT is earnings before interest and taxes.[93] It is a measurement of your business's profit that accounts for all income and expenses (operating and nonoperating), except interest and income tax expenses.

Creating a profitable business is the hard part. The easy part is to calculate what you can expect if you sell it. As an example, if your

---

93   Chris Murphey, "Earnings Before Interest and Taxes—EBIT," Investopedia, July 8, 2019, https://www.investopedia.com/terms/e/ebit.asp.

company has an annual cash flow of $100,000, your selling price will likely be between $250,000 and $450,000.

And if you want to think big, you can create a business model that you could franchise. Instead of selling once, you could essentially sell your business over and over. If you go in this direction, you'll be known as the franchisor. The individuals you would offer your concept to would be franchisees. Basically, you are selling your profitable business model to others. Because of the trials and tribulations you endured, combined with your experience and understanding of best practices within your organization and industry, others will be willing to pay a fee for this knowledge. Why? Because you figured out what works, and this minimizes risk for the franchisee.

The franchisee pays an up-front fee and often additional moneys based on revenue they create. The franchisee is responsible for all out-of-pocket expenses to open and operate their business. You are responsible (for a predetermined period of time) to train employees on how to market and sell the product or service. In addition, you supply (at no cost to you) business systems and processes while giving guidance and support for overall operations.

Are there other options? Absolutely. When you start something, you never know where it will end up. For example, fortune came to me. I started my business with a couple thousand dollars and little experience. But I had good instincts and learned a lot along the way. Before I was forty, the visual media company, Getty Images, Inc., approached me to acquire my company. Was I happy? No doubt. Did I take their first offer? No way. Just like I have told you, negotiate everything. They sweetened the pot, and I signed on the dotted line.

Two years later, Getty wanted to take a different direction and offered me the company back at a reduced price. Did I take the first offer? Nope. Eventually, I was able to acquire my company back for pennies on the dollar. Like I said, you just never know what will happen when you are dedicated, creative, innovative, and proactive.

Financial Literacy[94]

Let's make sure you're up to speed with some basic financial terms and definitions:

Accounting: A system that provides measurable information about finances.

Accounts payable (AP): Money owed by a business to its suppliers shown as a liability on a company's balance sheet.

Accounts receivable (AR): Money a company has a right to receive because it provided customers with goods and/or services.

Advertising: A means of communication with users or potential users of a product or service with the goal of making your product or service known to an audience or marketplace.

Assets: The value of everything a company owns and uses to conduct their business.

Balance sheet: A statement of the assets, liabilities, and capital of a business at a particular point in time, detailing the balance of income and expenditure over the preceding period.

Barter: An exchange of goods or services for other goods or services without using money.

Business plan: A document setting out a business's future objectives and strategies for achieving them.

Business: An organization that operates with the intention of making a profit.

---

94 Meredith Wood, "60 Business Finance Terms and Definitions You Absolutely Should Know," Fundera, August 3, 2019, https://www.fundera.com/blog/business-finance-terms-and-definitions.

Business to business (B2B): One business selling goods or services to another business.

Business to consumer (B2C): A business selling goods or services directly to the end user, also known as a retailer.

Cash flow (CF): Incoming and outgoing cash, representing the operating activities of an organization; in accounting, cash flow is the difference in amount of cash available at the beginning of a period (opening balance) and the amount at the end of that period (closing balance).

Collateral: Something pledged as security for repayment of a loan, to be forfeited in the event of a default.

Contract: A formal agreement to do work for pay.

CEO: A chief executive officer, the highest-ranking person in a company or other institution, ultimately responsible for making managerial decisions.

Credit score: Your creditworthiness.

Copyright: The exclusive, legal right given to an originator or an assignee to print, publish, perform, film, or record literary, artistic, or musical material and to authorize others to do the same.

Depreciation: The degrading value of an asset over time.

Distributor/supplier/vendor: Anyone who provides goods or services to a company or individuals.

Due diligence: A comprehensive appraisal of a business undertaken by a prospective buyer, especially to establish its assets and liabilities and evaluate its commercial potential.

EBIT: Earnings before interest and taxes.

Entrepreneur: Someone who organizes, manages, and takes on the risk of starting a new business.

Expense: Money spent on supplies, equipment, or other investments for your business.

Franchisee: One who purchases a franchise; the franchisee then runs that location of the purchased business and is responsible for certain decisions, while many other decisions (such as the look, name, and products) are already determined by the franchisor and must be kept the same by the franchisee. The franchisee will pay the franchisor under the terms of the agreement, either a flat fee or a percentage of the revenues or profits from the sales transacted at that location.

Franchisor: A person or company that grants the license to a third party for the conducting of a business under the franchisor's marks; the franchisor owns the overall rights and trademarks of the company and allows its franchisees to use these rights and trademarks to do business.

Incorporated/corporation: A company or other organization formed into a legal entity.

Income statement/profit and loss (P&L): One of the financial statements that shows you how much money your business earned and lost within a period of time.

Inflation: A general increase in prices and fall in the purchasing value of money.

Liabilities: The value of what a business owes.

Limited liability corporation (LLC): The US-specific form of a private limited company, a business structure that can combine the pass-through taxation of a partnership or sole proprietorship with the limited liability of a corporation.

Marketing: The process of promoting, selling, and distributing a product or service to the marketplace.

Net income/profit: Revenues minus expenses.

Net worth: All assets minus liabilities.

Profit: A financial gain, especially the difference between the amount earned and the amount spent in buying, operating, or producing something—also known as the "bottom line."

Profit margin: The ratio of profit divided by revenue displayed as a percentage. The formula to calculate the profit margin: First, find your gross profit, which is the difference between the revenue ($200) and the cost ($150), so $50. To find the margin, divide gross profit by the revenue (.25). To make the margin a percentage, multiply the result by 100. The margin is 25 percent.

Projections: A forecast of future revenues and expenses; typically, the projection will account for internal or historical data and will include a prediction of external market factors.

Return on investment (ROI): How much money a business gets in return from an investment.

Revenue: The entire amount of income before expenses are subtracted.

Sales prospect: A potential customer.

Trademark: A symbol, word, or words legally registered or established by use as representing a company or product.

Trade show: An exhibition at which businesses in a particular industry promote their products and services.

Target market: A specific group of customers at which a company aims its products and services.

Wholesaler: A person or company that sells goods in large quantities at low prices, typically to retailers. Typical wholesale discounts will range between 40-60 percent.

Personal Finances

As a millennial, you have a fantastic advantage when it comes to understanding money: you are young! Unfortunately, I have personally experienced and witnessed many financial meltdowns in close family members and friends—loved ones who didn't plan correctly or made a few mistakes along the way. And I'm not just talking about people who had average jobs. I am talking about doctors, lawyers, and even financial advisors who got mixed up along the way. Their homes, cars, and other assets were lost in the wreckage. Some went bankrupt; others were evicted due to lack of payment. The stress of financial concerns destroyed relationships and took a toll on their health. In some cases, a life-changing event they didn't see coming (and didn't save for) proved devastating. In others, the misfortune can be traced back to not having solid financial habits in place. They didn't save much, used debt as an instrument to pay expenses, and lived above their means.

My dad was the greatest guy in the world and a hardworking family man. He had a good job for more than twenty-five years with a pension, but then he decided to leave the company and work for someone else. We moved to Pennsylvania, and within six months, his new job let him go. We moved back to New York, and he was able to get his old job back, but they took his pension away. My parents then inherited a little money and decided to put our house up for collateral to start a business (a bakery). Dad didn't read the lease properly (he explained to me years later), so the expenses were much more than he anticipated. Within a year, his business went bankrupt. He was at the bakery at four o'clock each morning. He had a heart attack; then depression and low self-worth set in, and he never recovered after that. All it took was a few bad decisions to take away the decades of savings and wealth he had built.

This taught me, early on, how I did *not* want to live. I'm not saying you should be me, but throughout my life, I have had only three credit cards, and one was for business. Never would I pay a credit card statement late. Just look at the ridiculous fees these lenders charge! Sometimes it's as much as 24 percent.

As an example, if you had a $1,000 balance on your credit card with a 24 percent interest rate and you paid the minimum, it would take you 125 months (more than ten years) to be rid of your debt. So, what does this mean? Though you eventually paid off the $1,000, you also paid an additional $1,332.19 in interest. So, your original $1,000 debt cost you $2,332.19. I've seen people have $50,000 plus in credit debt. Do the numbers on that. It's scary. This is not a recipe for smart living.

Investment Advice

People often say, "It takes money to make money." Truth be told, that statement is often wrong. It takes experience and knowledge to make money. If you lack experience and knowledge, then it does take lots of money—and you take on lots of risk, still with no guarantee of success. But the more knowledge and experience you have, the less money you need and the fewer risks you have to take. That's why the rich get richer.

If you're looking for specific investment advice, I will leave that up to other authors. I would rather play the role of a mentor who has seen a lot of good and bad when it comes to how people handle money. Therefore, I'd like to share strategy and advice to stay out of debt and build wealth over a lifetime.

It takes experience and knowledge to make money . . . the more knowledge and experience you have, the less money you need and the fewer risks you have to take.

Let's talk about why you need to make money from the money you have and the profits that come in. According to the *Oxford Dictionary*, *inflation* is "a general increase in prices and fall in the purchasing value of money." In other words, as years pass, the price of a product will most likely increase. For example, a new house in 1975 might have cost $48,000, but because of inflation, a similar house in 2015 might be $270,200. A new car in 1975 was around $3,800, but in 2015, new car prices rose to around $31,252.[95]

According to the Bureau of Labor Statistics' consumer price index, the dollar experienced an average inflation rate of 3.68 percent per year from 1975 until 2015.[96] This may not seem like much per year, but when you add it up, prices in 2015 are 355.61 percent higher than prices in 1975. Inflation effects what it will cost you to buy goods and services.

Chances are, your best "investment" will be what you do for a living. The more desirable your skills and knowledge are to an employer, the better earning power you will have. So what do you invest in as you acquire wealth?

Not too long ago, I heard Warren Buffet's take on the "value" financial advisors and brokers bring to the table. He explained, when you hire a plumber, chances are, you will get your pipes fixed. If you hire an electrician, likely he will get your lights to work. But if you give your money to a financial broker, you're not going to get what you expect.[97] If you only put your money into a no-load (no fee) index fund, chances are, you would have made more money than giving to the experts.[98] These "financial gurus" are some of the wealthiest people in the world,

---

95 "Comparing the Cost of Living between 1975 and 2015," My Budget 360, http://www.mybudget360.com/cost-of-living-compare-1975-2015-inflation-price-changes-history/.

96 CPI Inflation Calculator, http://www.in2013dollars.com/1975-dollars-in-2017?amount=1.

97 "Buffet Says Money Spent on Plumbers Better Than on Hedge Funds," Personal Finance News, May 8, 2017, https://personalfinancenews.com/buffett-says-money-spent-on-plumbers-better-than-on-hedge-funds/.

98 Adam Barone, "No-Load Fund," Investopedia, April 23, 2019, https://www.investopedia.com/terms/n/no-loadfund.asp.

often making millions of dollars per year. Educate yourself before you turn your hard-earned money to others.

Do you think it would be a sure thing to make money on your investments if you had some of the most brilliant minds in the world looking after your funds? Not so fast. In 2018, "The 10-year returns achieved by the endowments (endowment investments have dual goals: to grow the principal and to generate income) for all the Ivy League schools lagged a plain-vanilla portfolio of stocks and bonds, according to a new study by Markov Processes International. The simulated portfolio is conservative, made up of 60 percent stocks and 40 percent bonds, and it achieved an annualized return of 8.1 percent. Not one Ivy League school beat that performance. A slightly more aggressive mix of 70 percent stocks and 30 percent bonds surpassed the Ivys' results by an even greater margin."[99]

Be careful of becoming a victim of "the greatest fool theory." This is when you are willing to pay a ridiculously high price because of the hype. You then have the hope and expectation that others will buy into the hype and the item will be resold to a "greater fool" later for an even higher price. The "bubble" then bursts, and people are no longer willing to fall for the hype. This leaves many with no outlet to sell what they thought was going to be a valuable investment. In many cases, if it seems too good to be true, it probably is.

If you can figure out a shortcut for achieving wealth, then, by all means, go for it. Plenty of "get rich quick" strategies are out there to choose from. Maybe some of them work; maybe a lot of them don't. Unfortunately, I was taken in by Bernard Madoff's scheme in 2008. Bernie had tremendous credibility as the former NASDAQ chairman. His fraud amounted to $64.8 billion. Lives were destroyed by this

---

99 Geraldine Fabrikant, "A College Investor Who Beats the Ivys," *The New York Times*, March 22, 2019, https://www.nytimes.com/2019/03/22/business/college-investor-who-beats-the-ivys.html.

criminal. I didn't have much with him, but what I did have, I've never received a dollar back.

My point is, avoid the trapdoors of investing. Be wary and careful; ask questions. It's okay to take risk, but don't be greedy. If you want to take a chance on a long shot, do it with a small percentage of your savings. If it works, you will feel good; if it doesn't work, you will have learned a valuable lesson and still have money in the bank.

Let me tell you what has served me well: front-loading my savings. Early on, in my twenties, I worked very hard and made a lot of money. Did I buy a few nice things? Yes, but not many. What I learned early on was a concept called compounding interest. Wikipedia explains it well: "Compound interest is the addition of interest to the principal sum of a loan or deposit or, in other words, interest on interest. It is the result of reinvesting interest, rather than paying it out, so that interest in the next period is then earned on the principal sum plus previously accumulated interest."[100] Albert Einstein has been quoted as saying, "Compound interest is the eighth wonder of the world. He who understands it, earns it . . . He who doesn't . . . pays it. Compound interest is the most powerful force in the universe."[101]

The Magic of Compounding

So, let's look at a simple example. Let's say you put away $50,000 and add an additional $10,000 per year. If you hold it for twenty years, your contributing funds would be $250,000.

If you had a conservative return of 6 percent (over the last ninety years, the S&P 500 has returned 9.8 percent a year after adjusting for

---

100 "Compound Interest," *Wikipedia* page, last updated July 25, 2019, https://en.wikipedia.org/wiki/Compound_interest.

101 Quora, https://www.quora.com/Albert-Einstein-famously-stated-%E2%80%9CCompound-interest-is-the-eighth-wonder-of-the-world-He-who-understands-it-earns-it-he-who-doesn%E2%80%99t-pays-it-%E2%80%9D-How-can-the-average-person-use-this.

inflation),[102] you would have a total value of $550,284—more than double what you put in. If you did the same for thirty years, you would have $1,125,191.33.[103]

Or, if, at the age of thirty, you invested $20,000 and never added any more money, in thirty years, when you're ready to retire, it would be worth $201,253 (using an 8 percent return—still lower than the average over ninety years). All you have to do is simply put the funds into a S&P index at age thirty.[104]

If you're under the age of thirty-five, you have one of the biggest advantages out there when it comes to planning for eventual financial freedom. How much you can put away per month is important, but that number pales in comparison to how much time you can invest in your plan. In other words, the sooner you start, the greater the advantage you'll have.

Don't Believe It?

Check out the chart below, which plots the savings strategies of three fictional investors, each of whom saved the same amount of money over a ten-year term. Through an incredible stroke of investment luck, each earned the same average annual return (7 percent) consistently, until age sixty-five. The only difference between these investors is the year they started socking away savings. If you ever plan to retire—and who doesn't—you should be amazed by the results.

---

102 Michael Santoli, "'The S&P 500 Has Already Met Its Average Return for a Full Year, but Don't Expect It to Stay Here," CNBC, June 18, 2017, https://www.cnbc.com/2017/06/18/the-sp-500-has-already-met-its-average-return-for-a-full-year.html.

103 Compound Interest Calculator, http://www.moneychimp.com/calculator/compound_interest_calculator.htm.

104 Alaina Tweddale, "If You Still Don't Believe in the Power of Compound Interest, You Have to See This," Money Under 30, April 29, 2019, https://www.moneyunder30.com/power-of-compound-interest.

The Data Doesn't Lie

Michael saved $1,000 per month from age twenty-five to thirty-five. Then he stopped saving but left his money in his investment account where it continued to accrue at a 7 percent interest rate until he retired at age sixty-five.

Jennifer held off and didn't start saving until age thirty-five. She put away $1,000 per month from age thirty-five to forty-five. Like Michael, she left the balance in her investment account where it continued to accrue at a rate of 7 percent interest until age sixty-five.

Sam didn't get around to investing until age forty-five. Still, he invested $1,000 per month for ten years, halting his savings at age fifty-five. Then he also left his money to accrue at a 7 percent interest rate until his sixty-fifth birthday.

Michael, Jennifer, and Sam each saved the same amount—$120,000—over a ten-year period. Sadly for Jennifer, and even more so for Sam, their ending balances were dramatically different.[105]

Saver	Ending Balance
Michael	$1,444,969
Jennifer	$734,549
Sam	$373,407

---

105 Ibid.

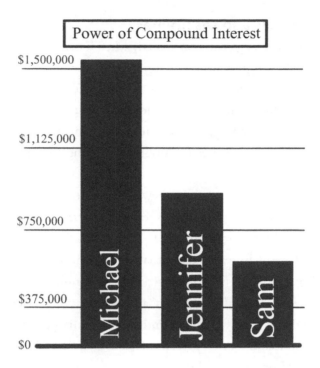

A fun way to figure out what your money will be worth after compounding is to use the compounding calculator at moneychimpcom.[106] Just plug in your own numbers and watch the magic happen.

This is what I am talking about: getting wealthy, strong and steady. The earlier you start, the bigger compounding effect you will enjoy. By the way, if you just had two less beers or alcohol drinks per week, you would save about $20 per week, $80 per month, $960 per year. Compounding this money over twenty years at 6 percent would give you $37,444; over thirty years, you would get $80,449.

---

106 Ibid.

Financial Goals and Disciplines

I am big on setting goals, particularly when it comes to my finances. Financial goals will provide you with focused discipline, a productive and beneficial direction that fuels your ambition to create a lifestyle you desire. Unfortunately, most educational systems don't focus on personal financial planning, but that's no excuse. You alone must assume responsibility for your financial position, and setting goals is one way to be responsible.

According to a report from Pew Charitable Trusts, 80 percent of Americans are in debt.[107] The average American household carries $137,063 in debt, according to the Federal Reserve's latest numbers.[108] Yet the US Census Bureau reports that the median household income was just $59,039 in 2016.[109] Sixty-two percent of millennials owe more in debt, overall, than they have in a personal savings account. The GOBankingRates survey, which identified millennials as ages nineteen to thirty-four, found that 67 percent had less than $1,000 in savings.[110]

You would be surprised how many people, when asked, have little or no clue as to their total monthly expenses and how much they bring home in income after taxes. If you fall into that category, change that apathetic mindset today. Start by tracking what you spend over a month's time. Many apps are available to help you track, but good, old-fashioned pen and pad works just as well. Next, what are your earnings after taxes?

---

107 "80% of Americans Are in Debt," Credit.com, August 3, 2015, https://blog.credit.com/2015/08/80-of-americans-are-in-debt-122255/.

108 Leo Sun, "A Foolish Take: Here's How Much Debt the Average U.S. Household Owes," USA Today, November 18, 2017, https://www.usatoday.com/story/money/personalfinance/2017/11/18/a-foolish-take-heres-how-much-debt-the-average-us-household-owes/107651700/.

109 "Income, Poverty, and Health Insurance Coverage in the United States: 2016," Newsroom, September 12, 2017, https://www.census.gov/newsroom/press-releases/2017/income-povery.html.

110 Kathleen Elkins, "A Growing Percentage of Millennials Have Absolutely Nothing Saved," CNBC, February 12, 2018, https://www.cnbc.com/2018/02/09/a-growing-percentage-of-millennials-have-absolutely-nothing-saved.html.

You can look at your pay stub to see what taxes are being deducted, or you can speak with the payroll company to calculate this number.

Now subtract what you are spending from what you are making after taxes, and this is your discretionary spending. Just like in a business, if you are spending more than you bring home, then you are heading in the wrong direction. Understand how much money you make after expenses and as simple as it sounds, don't spend more than you are making.

You would be surprised how many people, when asked, have little or no clue as to their total monthly expenses and how much they bring home in income after taxes.

Priority number one should be to pay off all debt, including your student debt. This comes before saving. Chances are, you are paying more interest than you can earn. You may think you can earn more, and that may be true in some cases, but the interest you are paying on your debt is a guaranteed expense you should not have.

Develop a realistic and sensible mindset. Don't be the person who focuses on what they don't have rather than what they do have. If you are always envious or preoccupied with lack, you will never find peace—no matter how much money you accumulate. Start young, and don't give in to peer pressure, looking at what "everybody else" is buying. You will see others with fancy cars or expensive toys, but just like social media, you don't see what's really going on behind closed doors with their finances.

I live in an affluent area where people spend money they don't have. The grief and pressure they put on themselves is constant and demoralizing. If they would only cut back, their lives could be much better. I have also seen people break the law because they wanted to keep up with their friends or neighbors. Yes, they were willing to commit fraud just to have more money to buy more things. Even if others can afford what you can't, don't value your success or your life by the material objects you have or don't have.

Learn to say no to more stuff—even if it means disappointing a spouse, girlfriend, or boyfriend. Be gentle but be firm that you have no interest in digging yourself into a financial mess. Try and get them on the same page as you. Discussing your common goals and future early on will dramatically reduce future money worries.

Yes, have a credit card to pay for items and establish your credit score (your creditworthiness), but always pay your credit card in full at the end of the month. If you don't have the money to pay for it, then you have spent too much and are not planning well. If you are late in paying your bills, it negatively affects your credit score. Credit scores range from 350-850 and may be referred to as a FICO score. FICO is an abbreviation for the Fair Isaac Corporation, the first company to offer a credit-risk model with a score. The score is a way to evaluate your credit worthiness.[111] A credit score between 580 to 669 is below average which could make it harder to get a loan, and your interest rates may be higher.[112]

Do your best to pay as you buy. In other words, pay for your item with cash, debit card, or check. If you have your eye on a costly item, save for it. Don't go into debt to buy it now. Do thorough research to make sure you are getting a fair deal. As far as I am concerned, most high-ticket items should be negotiated. I have never paid the asking price for a house, car, washer and dryer, or even an emergency veterinarian visit. Just simply say, "I'm sorry. I can't afford that," or "Can you offer a

---

111 "What Does FICO Stand For?," Dictionary.com, https://www.dictionary.com/e/fico-credit-score/.

112 Kevin Outllaw, "What Is a Good FICO Score?," Bankrate, January 11, 2017, https://www.bankrate.com/finance/credit/what-is-good-fico-score.aspx.

better price?" Then don't say a word after your statement and watch how quickly they will drop the price.

Make sure you have medical coverage in place. One of the best ways to go broke is an unexpected medical expense. Over 60 percent of all bankruptcies are due to medical expenses. According to healthcare.gov, a typical inpatient stay in a hospital is about three days, and that may cost you over $30,000.[113] This figure may not even include major procedures, ambulance fees, or other charges. Look into a health savings account (HSA), which can be a nice way to save on your taxes come year-end.

Save as much as you can, particularly if you live at home with your parents and your overhead is low. Why? Because before you know it, you will be living outside the home you grew up in, and expenses will increase. Save as much as you can as early as you can.

If your company offers a 401(k) match, max it out. According to the Bureau of Labor Statistics, the typical or average 401(k) match nets out to 3.5 percent.[114] Half of employers will match employee contributions between 0-6 percent of salary. In other words, your employer will give you free money, assuming they have a match plan in place. Each month you will be adding to your retirement plan, and you can enjoy great tax-deferred savings as well.

Sit with an accountant. Make sure you are taking all legitimate deductions and keeping track of charitable contributions for tax purposes. Document everything. If you get it wrong and you are audited, you will need to pay what you owe and a penalty.

Uncertainty is certain. Have an emergency fund in place. How much? How about enough money to carry your overhead for three to

---

113 "Protection from High Medical Costs," Healthcare.gov, https://www.healthcare.gov/why-coverage-is-important/protection-from-high-medical-costs/.

114 G.E. Miller, "Does Your 401K Match up against the Averages?," 20 Something Finance, January 13, 2019, https://20somethingfinance.com/401k-match/.

six months. You may lose your job, but having an emergency fund will reduce desperation and give you time to land on your feat.

I am not saying to be overly frugal, cheap, or stingy, but be careful and prudent. Think it over before you commit to the purchase. Are you going to be able to pay, or will you have regret when the bill comes due? I have a brilliant fourteen-year-old daughter. Emma happens to be a straight-A student and wise to the ways of the world. We had a conversation about buying brands: handbags, jewelry, and watches from Louis Vuitton, Gucci, and Rolex. We both agreed it's a sucker's game. (My words, not hers.) If you buy these brands to make yourself feel special or important, as far as I am concerned, you have your priorities in the wrong place. Sacrificing future savings for status symbols is a fool's game. I hope Emma feels the same way in her twenties.

If you have a financial setback from spending too much, stop before it gets worse. Try and make up for it in the coming months. Certainly, a great fix is to increase your income. When I was a kid, I often worked two to three jobs at a time. Sure it was hard, but it started me on the right path. I never got into debt, never had to borrow from others, and eventually arrived at the lifestyle I wanted.

If you're doing a good job, don't be afraid to ask for a raise. If you're not doing a good job, step it up. Be the first in and last out; go beyond your job description. Believe me, the boss is always watching.

Hesitate when committing to recurring monthly bills. Big companies are making a fortune off the public a few dollars at a time. Do the math for what it will cost month after month, year after year, for the subscription service or membership that automatically debits your account. It all adds up.

Stop with the impulse items. If you don't need it, don't buy it. If you're buying things to make yourself feel better emotionally, stop and ask yourself if this is the best way to get relief. Find relief in something else, like setting goals at the gym, learning a new hobby, or maybe even seeking out a counselor to talk to.

As you accumulate wealth, have an umbrella policy in place. Investopedia describes an umbrella insurance policy as extra liability insurance coverage that goes beyond the limits of the insured's home, auto, or watercraft insurance.[115] It provides an additional layer of security to those who are at risk for being sued for damages to other people's property or injuries caused to others in an accident. It also protects against libel, vandalism, slander, and invasion of privacy. An umbrella insurance policy is very helpful when the insurance owner is sued and the dollar limit of the original policy has been exhausted. The added coverage provided by liability insurance is most useful to individuals who own a lot of assets or very expensive assets and are at significant risk for being sued.

Be patient and focused. Be resilient during difficult financial times. Change your lifestyle when needed. I have written a lot about discipline, no doubt, but you are going to have to deal with money matters your entire life. The sooner you understand how to avoid the pitfalls of poor money management, the more you will be in control of your future.

---

115 Julia Kagan, "Umbrella Insurance Policy," Investopedia, February 11, 2018, https://www.investopedia.com/terms/u/umbrella-insurance-policy.asp.

CONCLUSION
You're More Than a Millennial—
Much More

Rather than writing a traditional conclusion, I wrote a letter of encouragement and advice to my millennial friends. Why? Because you are much more than a millennial, and I am excited for your future.

Aim high with your aspirations and goals and be willing to put in the work to achieve them. Your age group holds much potential. In fact, UBS reports millennials could be worth up to $24 trillion by 2020.[116] But don't act like you're entitled to success. Instead, maintain an unwavering work ethic. Always have a sense of urgency to get the job done. If you accept half-ass effort from yourself, you'll get the same caliber of results. Remember, others have the same ambitions you do. Don't lose out because of lack of effort.

Don't buy the lie that success happens overnight. The countless stories you've heard about "overnight success" are actually about people who consistently followed a series of small steps in the right direction until they achieved their dreams. Building success is about seeing the barely noticeable little doors, perhaps opened just a crack, as a pathway

---

116 Thomas Franck, UBS Reports Millennials Could Be Worth Up to $24 Trillion by 2020," CNBC, June 23, 2017, https://www.cnbc.com/2017/06/23/ubs-millennials-worth-24-trillion-by-2020.html.

to fulfilling your dream. Achieving success isn't a "spectator sport." You must be an active participant; success is earned, not given.

As you navigate life, understand failure is never final unless you let it be. Just look at the lion. When a lion hunts its prey, it misses three out of four times, yet it is still called "king of the jungle."[117] Persevere and *you* can be the king of the jungle too.

Or consider the average MLB Hall of Famer batting average of .303.[118] Seven out of ten times at bat, he fails to get a hit, yet he is still considered one of the best ballplayers ever to live. Don't give up when you don't succeed with your first attempt. We are all a work in progress, so set a goal to develop a better version of yourself each day. Learn from setbacks and figure out new ways to succeed and move forward. Once you understand the process of finding solutions, maneuvering through life will be that much easier.

Devote yourself to optimism. Look for the good in the world. I see plenty of it. Learn to bounce back from disappointments. Poet Maya Angelou articulates such optimism in this line: "This is a wonderful day. I have never seen this one before."

Looking back on my career and life, I can say I have been more consistent and proactive than most. Consistency comes into play each day as I defeat procrastination and do what needs to be done. Being proactive means that if I have a goal, I do my best to put self-doubt and fear on the side to pursue it. If I fail, I still know that failing is better than not trying at all. Take action and see your goals through to the end. If you come up short, don't let it be because you quit too soon.

---

117 James Fair, "Hunting Success Rates: How Predators Compare," Discover Wildlife, https://www.discoverwildlife.com/animal-facts/mammals/hunting-success-rates-how-predators-compare/.

118 Ross Carey, "Your Average Hall of Famer," Replacement Level Podcast, July 22, 2012, https://www.replacementlevelpodcast.com/2012/07/22/your-average-hall-of-famer/.

Continue to learn throughout your life. Even if it's through a hobby, keep your brain active, and you will stay young at heart. If you want to learn something, don't hesitate to seek out advice.

Don't just drift through life; it's okay to be a rebel. No need to conform to what others say you should do. Don't give in to the pressure of societal expectations. Why pursue what society tries to impose? You are unique, so make your mark. Prove the naysayers wrong. Be calculated and strategic but also create the life you desire. Don't let any person define who you are except you.

The most important relationship you will have in life is the one with yourself. Self-acceptance is crucial. Mistakes will happen, so determine to forgive yourself and others. We all have strengths and weaknesses. Focus on your strengths. We sometimes live in a "gotcha ya'" society. Do your best not to settle into the victim mindset. And, just as important, don't be a person always on the attack.

Make your mental health and fitness a priority. It will pay off for decades to come and insulate you against difficult times. Find an activity that allows you to push yourself beyond your limits and prove you are stronger than you realize. Then bring that tough mental mindset to your daily obstacles—especially when adversity hits. The goal is to take down self-imposed walls and push past former limits. I use exercise. I push myself past my breaking point during my workout each morning, and that helps me stay strong throughout the day. Exercise may not be your calling, but find a personal limit to push through and notice a stronger mindset develop.

Work on your coping skills as the ability to cope is paramount. Life will throw many unforeseen situations at you, so research how to deal with adversity. Seek professional help, if needed. Don't feel shame in reaching out if you're overwhelmed.

The need to have a purpose, not just responsibilities, is also crucial. At the end of each day, name something you are excited about, a reason to look forward to the next day. Stay humble. The more grounded you are, the better you will deal with life's twist and turns.

Surround yourself with optimistic people and those who truly have your best interests at heart. We all need encouragement. Avoid anything online that promotes self-doubt. Stay hungry and assume personal accountability for your own success. Look for help when you need it; accept help when it's offered. But in the end, it's up to you to make the most of each opportunity.

Have you ever been treated unjustly? To an extent, most of us have. I grew up in the 1970s when bullying was an everyday event. I was physically and mentally abused for just about any reason. I finally had enough. I was tired of others taking away my dignity and pride because I would not defend myself. I learned how to channel the negative emotions I felt into the determination to stand up for myself. I have several African American friends who were not given equal opportunity because of their skin color. They used this injustice as fuel to propel them toward their goals. Leonard Marshall, my good friend and two-time New York Giants Super Bowl champion and three-time all-pro NFL player, said it well: "Beat the odds by turning negative situations into massive motivating tools. Don't let negativity slow you down; instead, use it to push even harder and farther."

Be on a quest to reduce bad habits you may have. Bad habits can lead to unintentional consequences—outcomes that are not foreseen. I remember working in the bars as a bouncer. I would have my hands folded on my chest as I leaned against five-foot speakers. The music blasted, and I gave very little thought to the long-term effect it might have on my hearing. Now, one of my ears has about half the hearing capacity as the other. If you do things consistently that are not good for you, the potential for a long-term negative effect increases. A single mistake doesn't make a trend, but be careful not to string too many together.

Adopt high values, and you will sleep better at night. If you don't, one day you'll reflect back on your life and wish you had been a better person. With high values, you'll grow to have less concern about what people think about your appearance. It's ironic. When we're young and good-looking, the self-doubt we have regarding our appearance and how we carry ourselves can be overwhelming. Yet, when we get a bit older and our looks fade, many of us could care less what others think. The maturity principle is one reason for this change.[119] I like the way it is described on Social Psych Online: "The idea is that early in life, we're confused about where we fit into the grand scheme of society. As we get older, though, we start to adapt to social roles and understand our place. In doing so, we get more comfortable, confident, and capable."[120]

A great example of this is my son, Austin, who is a millennial. During his high school days, he was full of worry and a host of other insecurities: *What are others thinking of me? Are my grads good enough to get into college?* As he reflects back, he now laughs and realizes, *Why should I worry today when I won't even remember what I worried about a year from now?* He is evolving each day, trying to put life into prospective. He recently told me, "I'm being grateful and understanding I have the power to decide how I handle each situation . . . Fault and responsibility don't go together. It's not always somebody's fault (if X happens), but it's for damn sure that it's their responsibility to figure out how to find solutions when things go wrong."

I'm not talking about disregarding close relationships or dismissing how family and friends experience us. If "inner circle" relationships are

119 Avshalom Caspi, Brent W. Roberts, and Rebecca L. Shiner, "Personality Development: Stability and Change," Annual Review of Psychology, 2005, https://pdfs.semanticscholar.org/6d30/69890e986686aa4ff4ce5b4fcf404831cb2b.pdf.

120 "Self-Esteem Development Over Time: The Maturity Hypothesis," Social Psych Online, July 24, 2015, http://socialpsychonline.com/2015/07/self-esteem-development-over-the-maturity-hypothesis/.

broken and need to be fixed, then do your best to mend them. I'm talking about going into public places, stores, supermarkets, or just a crowd and being free from caring what others might think of you. After all, you don't really know what they are thinking in the first place. More important, opinions of people who know nothing about you shouldn't matter. Release this insecurity and gain a sense of power and freedom.

Don't compete with the guy or girl next door or compare what they have to what you don't. You will never win that game. Someone will always have more "things" than you. Focus on the many blessings you do have.

Don't be quick to judge others. Rather, try to understand different points of view. It's about the Golden Rule: "Do unto others as you would have them do unto you." This philosophy dates backs many thousands of years but is still relevant today.

Make self-discovery and growth a priority. Be willing to take on challenges and learn how to fly over life's hurdles. Get off the sidelines and take action to accomplish all you desire. Fight strong and hard for your happiness and success. It's worth it.

After reading this book, I hope you walk away with a renewed vision and a new can-do attitude. I want you to see a bigger picture and a brighter future for yourself—far greater than you had previously imagined. You will no longer allow your circumstances, your lack of resources, or your past to define who you are or what you can become. The best is truly yet to come.

ABOUT THE AUTHOR

Bestselling Author Jerry Gladstone is highly regarded in the self-development industry as a speaker and success coach.

At the age of twenty-six he founded a small fine art company and grew it into an international business that specialized in the production, distribution, and marketing of a wide variety of entertainment fine art. Jerry's business associations have given him unique access to movie studios and celebrities including 20th Century Fox, The Walt Disney Company, Warner Bros., DreamWorks SKG, Apple Corps Limited, Jim Davis' Garfield, Elvis Presley Enterprises, Frank Sinatra Enterprises, HBO, Sony, United Media, MGM, and Getty Images, among others.

In conversations with "Rocky" himself, Sylvester Stallone, and other super achievers, Jerry observed a "Common Thread" to success that inspired him to author his first book, *The Common Thread of Overcoming Adversity and Living Your Dreams*. Over the years Jerry has spent a significant amount of time interacting with and interviewing Academy Award and Grammy winners, Super Bowl and World Series champions, Rock & Roll Hall of Fame legends, Olympians, and boxing and UFC World Champions.

Jerry was born in Brooklyn, New York, and raised in Long Island. He and his wife, Brooke, currently live in Florida with their three children, Austin, Allie, and Emma. Jerry experienced low self-esteem and self-doubt and struggled academically as a youngster, but through his parents and sports, he learned that determination, dedication, and perseverance is a winning recipe for success.

Jerry is available for keynote speeches,
business coaching and life coaching services.
To learn more please visit JerryGladstone.com